Iconic ———————
SAN FRANCISCO
Dishes, Drinks & Desserts

Iconic ——————

SAN FRANCISCO

Dishes, Drinks & Desserts

LAURA SMITH BORRMAN

FEATURING PHOTOGRAPHY BY BRANDON BORRMAN

AMERICAN PALATE

Published by American Palate
A Division of The History Press
Charleston, SC
www.historypress.com

Front cover, top: Palace Hotel crab salad with green goddess dressing. *Palace Hotel*; *middle*: classic San Francisco cocktails; *bottom, left to right*: the It's It ice cream sandwich, Mission burrito and sourdough bread. *Brandon Borrman.*

First published 2018

ISBN 9781540235657

Library of Congress Control Number: 2018940078

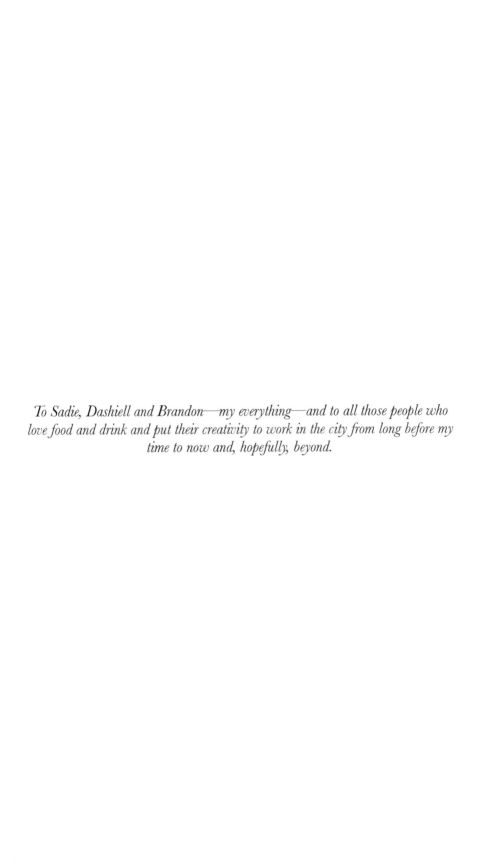

To Sadie, Dashiell and Brandon—my everything—and to all those people who love food and drink and put their creativity to work in the city from long before my time to now and, hopefully, beyond.

CONTENTS

CONTENTS

ACKNOWLEDGEMENTS

Exploring food and drink history brings a lot of passionate people out of the woodwork—or, rather, gorgeous antique backbars, electric dining rooms, revered libraries and historical societies, for this book, throughout Northern California. Bar historians, culinary academics, industry professionals, collectors, lovers of San Francisco and folks who just like to eat and have a good time—they all made this book possible. Thank you to Martin Cate, Erica Peters, Brandon Jew, Peter Quartaroli, Eric Passetti, Gio Costabile, Nico Vera, Jonathan Kauffman, Gary Ono, the folks at Anchor Brewing, Jennifer Puccio, Emily Luchetti, Thomas Rimpel, Gena Egelston, Iñaki Arrieta Baro, the Shamieh family (especially Charlie, Paul and Lana), Jenny Hodge, Emma Rowland, Carol Jensen, John Burton, Carter Wilson, Tamir Ben-Shalom, Marie Duggan, Brian Means, Cori Tahara and Michael Schaier, Jamie Law, Monica Carbone, Kathleen Correia, Jeff Thomas, Christina Moretta, Taryn Edwards, Laurie Krill, Hilary Parrish, Mike Buhler, Renee Roberts, the San Francisco Westerners Corral, the California State Library, the San Francisco Public Library, Lauren Thor, Josey Baker, Cathy Goldsmith, Andrew Meltzer, Valter Fabiano, Ian Adams, Michael Mina, Chris Cosentino, Julie Ho and Marcia Gagliardi. Thanks to my family: Roberta and Calvin Smith, Emily Smith, Jerry Chang and the Borrmans, Shiboskis and Kotzens. To my kids, Sadie and Dashiell, thank you for balancing my thrilling research with the important, exhilarating mundane and giving awesome snuggles. Thank you most of all to my husband, Brandon, whose talent with a camera and mutual love of food and drink continues to lead us into exciting projects together. Like life.

A NOTE ON ORIGIN STORIES AND ERAS

T hat's a sweet story they have in Martinez, but I think it's a bunch of hooey," a bar historian told me of the origins of the martini. "New York has a much stronger claim. I hope you include that."

Assuring him I would reference it, it was a moment that encapsulated much of the research for this book.

When you are writing a history book, even loosely, there is immense pressure to be sure you're capturing history. That may sound ridiculous, because of course, *it's history, no duh*, but what that means is there is pressure to ensure absolute accuracy, undoubtable, undeniable, factual retelling of what happened before you—likely long before you. It means citations and permissions, it means copyright clearances and historical collections, it means a black-and-white accounting of reality. It also means many, many opinions about what the truth really is.

Take the martini, for example. At a minimum, there are three competing and equitably valid origin stories for this famous drink. Three. I thought doing the research on the book would reveal a clear winner among all the myths. But no; what the research has revealed is multiple passionate, well-informed and differing accounts of how the king of cocktails came to be. (Though I do have a favorite. And it's a sweet one.)

I learned that writing a book about history is also about acceptance that the "real story" may not be ultimately discerned definitively but might rather be an amalgam of them all. And it's understandable that many people want to claim the rights to the history of famous foods and drinks because, why not,

THEY ARE AWESOME. The slate of cocktails and dishes and treats that compose this book are one-of-a-kind, legendary and truly (even if arguably) of a San Francisco spirit.

In the following pages, I will do my best to portray the myriad legends and accounts of what came before, to pay reverence to the historical truth as we honor the modern realizations of these wonderful foods and drinks of the City by the Bay. They are each legendary in their own right and, for the most part, have flourished in the modern cultural landscape of San Francisco. A few are difficult to find on modern menus but are, in fact, discoverable—and once discovered, they delight the palate in the way I'd like to think their creators intended.

Peruse the pages with a healthy appreciation for tall tales and enthusiastic storytellers and desirous claims to fame over the centuries. These are the facts, ma'am, as best as I was able to collect them.

So...What Is This Book?

San Francisco has long been an iconic city—for its centrality in great moments of American history, its resilience in the face of disaster, its position on the cutting edge of technology and its status as a focal point for major sociopolitical movements. And the city's food is no exception to its list of distinguishing features. Today, modern restaurants and bars in the city dominate the national and international culinary scene, often the feature of food magazine spreads and honorees in global competitions. But the city's food and drink has long been something special—with a handful of classic dishes still influencing the dining landscape today, each with a remarkable history of its own.

Iconic San Francisco Dishes, Drinks & Desserts captures the unique foods and drinks whose origins are inextricably linked to elements of the city's history, whether those be periods such as the gold rush or famous long-lost restaurants. These dishes, snacks and drinks have shaped the culinary consciousness of the magical city of many hills, and most of them remain prominent elements of the dining scene today, though many restaurants that once served them or fairs that made them most famous are long gone. This book will profile the foods, restaurants, people and historical moments to which they are tied and share recipes—some historical, some modern—for their creation at home.

Thar's Gold in Them Thar Hills!

San Francisco has been shaped by and persisted through adventure and adversity, starting with a golden moment just a couple hundred miles to the east. The town where it all began, Coloma, just east of Sacramento in the foothills, documents how a fleck of gold in the water changed the course of California's history—and population—forever:

> *On January 24, 1848, an event occurred in Coloma that would radically impact the history of California and the nation. James W. Marshall was building a sawmill for Captain John Sutter, using water from the South Fork of the American River. He noticed several flakes of metal in the tailrace water and recognized them to be gold. Though he tried to keep it a secret, the word spread quickly, and triggered the California Gold Rush of 1849.*
>
> *Some 80,000 immigrants poured into California during 1849. By the 1850s miners were coming from places all over the world—Britain, Europe, China, Australia, North and South America.*
>
> *After the gold petered out, many weary miners headed home. But others took a second look at California and liked what they saw. These hearty pioneers found the land unbelievably productive, and ultimately California's great wealth came not from its mines but from its farms. California, with its diverse population, achieved statehood in 1850, decades earlier than it would have been without the gold.*[1]

Gold brought miners and more: bakers, entrepreneurs, immigrants looking for a better life. They set up shop and put down roots along the gold rush routes of Northern California, changing the shape and look of the then territory's population (it ballooned from about 1,000 before 1848 to 100,000 by the end of 1849).[2]

> *"Ironically the great breakthrough of the Gold Rush was not creating fortunes from this precious metal found in the hills of California, it was essentially the invention of California itself," said author and historian Steven Johnson on a History Channel special about the phenomenon. "It made this extraordinary city of San Francisco, and got enough people to move all the way out there that the state was able to turn into this kind of extraordinary creature that it is today."*[3]

Bill of fare from popular San Francisco gold rush–era hotel the Ward House, 1849. *California History Room, California State Library, Sacramento, California.*

This seminal event both sped up California's admittance into the Union and left a lot of people in its wake, as destitute miners became commonplace and the "rush" slowed. In 1854, an important organization formed in San Francisco to fill the void and help lift and focus the working class: the Mechanics' Institute. Taryn Edwards, brilliant librarian and strategic partnerships manager at today's Mechanics' Institute Library and Chess Room on Post Street, and a historian herself, shares that the institute "aimed to be a school of technology, a library and lecture hall for the educational advancement of the working class—a group sorely in need of such an organization." Edwards explains the mind-set of the institute founders: all had "boundless faith in the future of San Francisco as a port and industrial center; concern about the moral atmosphere of San Francisco—all the casinos, saloons, and sporting houses that made up the bulk of the City's entertainment options were not conducive to a healthy society; and most importantly had an intense aversion to imported goods, which they believed kept prices high and deprived local people of jobs."[4]

Edwards has researched extensively some of the city's most important historical figures, but I mention her today for her studies on the Mechanics fairs, which became launch pads for some of San Francisco's most famous foods and drinks. The fairs started as a way to raise money for the institute—to support classes, purchase library materials and promote the town in general. So they copied the "international exposition" concept in place at other cities and organized an event to show off the best, most interesting goings-on in San Francisco.

"The concept of 'buy local' in California is not new," Edwards shares. "In the 1850s it was just as important because there was very little industry [in the region]. With its economy completely tied to the production of gold—a source of capital that fluctuated wildly—most goods had to be imported at incredible cost."[5]

Thirty-one Mechanics fairs were held between 1857 and 1899, and the city's best local goods—including coffee, beer, wine, bread and chocolate—figured prominently in the exhibitions. Edwards continues: "Many products that you all know and love debuted at our fairs, including cable cars, Levi Strauss's riveted pants, Folgers & Hills Brothers Coffees, Ghirardelli and Guittard chocolates, Martinelli's cider…and Boudin Bread."

The penchant for the local and freshly made—with the exception of a canned food obsession in the middle of the next century—has remained strong in the region. Culinary historian Erica Peters touches on this in her wonderful work *San Francisco: A Food Biography* (2013) and discusses how cookbooks have chronicled various moments in the city's—and state's—history, showing the way in which fresh ingredients were both revered and rejected and revered again. Looking at these old cookbooks and their sometimes-arcane recipes, it also becomes clear how diverse and divergent cultures can share a surprising lot when it comes to ingredients and structural profiles of food. L.L. McLaren describes this in *The Pan-Pacific Cook Book: Savory Bits from the World's Fare* (1915), which reads like an international fusion book before that was a thing:

> *In our cosmopolitan San Francisco we have singular opportunities of varying the monotony of our menus, and, in epitomizing this collection, I have been struck with the divergencies in preparations which contain the same ingredients. It is no less remarkable that in cookery as in folklore striking resemblances can be found in races remote from each other in space, origin and language.*

And perhaps it's these "striking resemblances" that have held together and distinguished the city's food scene over the decades. There's historically been both a blending of cultures and a drawing of lines—a simultaneous celebration of oneness and honoring of specific cultural traditions. Both a coming and going of immigrants and native San Franciscans (many of whom once started as immigrants), given the city's bayside locale and gateway to the rest of the world. A togetherness and spirit of individualism all at once.

The 1915 Panama-Pacific International Exposition marked by the cookbook signaled the rebirth of the city after its devastating great earthquake and fire nearly ten years earlier. It brought together exhibitors from all walks of life and disciplines and showed off the city's diverse population, culture and products: the kitchen sink dish of the Chinese; a seafood stew of Italian

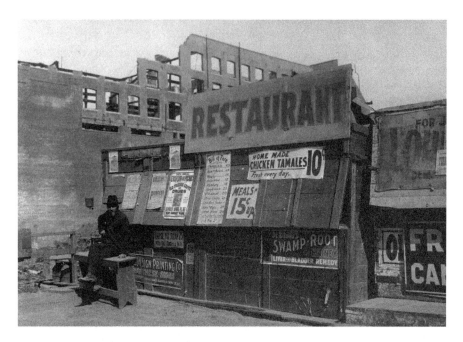

Makeshift box restaurant in San Francisco, 1907. From the book *San Francisco Earthquake and Fire 1906. California History Room, California State Library, Sacramento, California.*

San Francisco saloon interior, circa 1909. *California History Room, California State Library, Sacramento, California.*

immigrant fishermen; tangy bread of French bakers. The immigrant story was pervasive in the city's narrative then and continues to this day.

As does its spirit of resilience. The city sustained the Great Depression and transformed into a military town through World War II, as the population in uniform swelled and U.S. naval ships dominated the ports. Families—even one profiled in this book—were touched by a contagion of fear, and some Japanese Americans were forced to close their businesses while they were held in internment camps and treated as a threat to the country. But once released, they returned to and rebuilt their lives, reopened their shops and continued making some of the city's most special food products, like fortune cookies and manju.

And what's good food without a proper drink? San Francisco's arguably most important cocktails are just as tied to the city's historical periods, with drinks born out of a fervor for notable bartenders (the Boothby) and gold mining legends (the martini—very arguably) and to capture the essence of other places (Picon punch, pisco punch, Irish coffee…). Prohibition shuttered official doors and opened secret drinking spots and speakeasies through the 1920s and into the early '30s, but the cocktail culture came back. Its strength today is undeniable, with star mixologists added to culinary slates alongside star chefs.

Throughout the writing of this work, I drank martinis for extra inspiration and discovered a lot of amazing people in the culinary world who are keeping these classic dishes (and a few treats) alive. I hope after reading you are as inspired as I was to get out there and taste, imbibe and listen to stories of the City by the Bay.

Chapter 1

SOURDOUGH BREAD:
IT'S SCIENCE, IT'S MAGIC, IT'S SAN FRANCISCO

(Gold Rush + Great 'Quake, 1906)

The staff of life, the thing my kids will always eat, dependable belly filler and early personal love of San Francisco's food scene: sourdough bread. Sourdough is quite possibly one of the most iconic of the city's foods— and one of the most accessible. It graces the tables of most every seafood restaurant in the city; it's available in bowl form in cafés throughout the Bay Area (and across the country), holding another culinary icon (clam chowder); and it can even be shipped around the world by the city's powerhouse purveyor of the stuff, Boudin Bakery. For a food that's one of the oldest around, it's become a bit of a cult phenomenon in the early twenty-first century, with individual bakers morphing into local superstars, known by first name or in direct association with the name of their bakery and being talked about by other icons of cookery and homemaking like Martha Stewart. And in other smaller local bakeries, some of which are just as if not more famous, and for a much longer time, the bread is quietly, artisanally, lovingly crafted by hand and served only to waiting customers, never shipped, never preserved in any modern way. And yet, even its origins are—sometimes hotly—disputed among residents.

The city's "continuously operating oldest business," Boudin has a strong story about how sourdough bread came to be in town. French immigrant baker Isidore Boudin established the business in 1849, the year of the gold rush; the company says, "It's believed that Isidore Boudin received the mother dough from one of these 49ers." The business grew over the years, and Boudin stuck to its mother-dough methods, baking breads using a wild yeast starter (composed of just flour, water and air) despite the introduction of commercial yeast. In 1873, Isidore married Louise Enri, who later would become the company's ruling matriarch after her husband's death. Then in 1906, she became its savior, tossing Boudin's precious starter into a bucket and fleeing the burning building after the big earthquake, not unlike one would do with a wedding album or heirloom jewelry.

On that gold rush connection, many believe that sourdough was originally crafted by miners panning local Northern California waterways. Without a steady supply of foodstuffs and resources, they allegedly relied on the nonperishable ingredients they could get—flour and water—and thus a beautiful bread was born.

There is proof of miners making bread, but culinary historian Erica Peters points out that it's difficult to document taste with much degree of historical accuracy, so it's tricky to know for sure how sour that bread was. She also explains that many of the miners in California did in fact have access to supply routes via trading posts and that commercial products for leavening and simplifying baking, such as baking soda, had already been introduced earlier that century, and miners were eager to take advantage of them. Peters quotes this description by one miner of how he baked his bread:

> *Taking a tin pan, which served alternately as a gold-washer and a bread-tray, I turned into it a few pounds of flour a small solution of saleratus* [baking soda], *and a few quarts of water, and then went to work in it with my hands, mixing it up and adding flour till I got it to the right consistency; then shaping it into a loaf, raked open the embers, and rolled it in, covering it with the live coals....In half an hour or so my bread was baked...a little burnt on one side, and somewhat puffed up, like the expectations of the gold-digger in the morning.*[6]

Peters brilliantly points out that there was in fact another gold rush, a few years later and a little farther north: the Klondike Gold Rush in Canada and Alaska. Here, she says, the miners were "isolated for months at a time. They survived by letting flour ferment or 'sour' over time, or by preserving starters in special pots worn on the body to keep the starter from freezing. These Alaskan miners earned the nickname 'sour doughs.' San Franciscans welcomed them warmly for the Mining Fair [in 1898...which] showcased San Francisco as a jumping-off point for miners headed to the Klondike and encouraged investment in California's own mining industry."[7]

Sourdough bread, miner style, date unknown. *Special Collections, UC Davis Library, Eastman Originals Collection.*

Naturally, as is the case at many exhibitions and fairs showing off the artisanry of locals and participants from afar, there was a food demonstration area. Called the Klondike Kitchen, it was the place people could learn how to make sourdough bread. Peters theorizes that this was the likely point of confusion between the two different miner groups and what explains the bleed of the term "sourdough" into San Franciscans' consciousness. It was only in the early twentieth century that written references to the sourness of certain San Francisco breads made their way to print.

Whatever the truest origin story, sourdough through the twentieth century became synonymous with San Francisco—and the fervor around bread in general has only deepened in the twenty-first century. Colombo, Parisian and Toscana bakeries were all regional peers and sourdough purveyors through the 1900s, with devoted fans of their own, eventually unifying as the San Francisco French Bread Company, ultimately to be sold (and shuttered) under the Wonder/Hostess group in the late 1990s. Before that, late midcentury saw a lot of activity in East Bay–produced artisanal breads, with Berkeley as ground zero. The Cheese Board Collective started in 1967 as a cheese shop with a unique approach to business: it was owned and operated by the workers, with each employee doing a bit of everything. Gradually, the collective expanded into bread when a customer came in and suggested his bread be sold along with the cheeses on offer. The collective said sure, sold that customer's bread and eventually decided to make its own. Around the same time, Chez Panisse opened.

"There was a real synergy between the two businesses, a lot of cultural exchange back and forth," explains Cathy Goldsmith, longtime member of the Cheese Board Collective, as she describes the evolution of the Cheese Board alongside that of Alice Waters's palace of locally farmed goodness, organic love and beautiful California cuisine.

About a decade later, Acme began, as many culinary stories do in the East Bay, as an outgrowth of Chez Panisse. Acme's founder, Steven Sullivan, had once baked breads for the restaurant and, after a trip to Europe with his wife, Suzie, was inspired by the natural leavening process, using naturally occurring wild yeasts instead of artificial leaveners. Upon their return, that inspiration led to a new business devoted to bread baking for local restaurants.

Goldsmith gave me a window into the time of the early 1970s and then '80s when several small food businesses located in a little patch of Berkeley, California, were all working not so much in competition but in support of one another's missions: to offer good food and a from-scratch (or the farm) experience to their patrons each day.

Both modeled after European traditions of slow food, daily customers, individually crafted products and sheer reverence for the process of food making, Cheese Board and Acme both make gorgeous breads and have paved the way for the new slate of bread makers in the area. And though they were some of the first in the area to approach bread making this way, now it seems like the natural leavening approach is the only way.

"I don't know of any of the serious bakers in the Bay Area—and there are more and more and more—who don't think that natural leavening and sourdough baking is among the most important things they do," said Steven Sullivan in 2015.[8]

Cathy Goldsmith has been at the Cheese Board for twenty-two years, serving as its community liaison, dough maker on Fridays, principal cookbook writer and many more roles over her time there.

When Cheese Board started to explore sourdough in the early 1970s, Goldsmith said, "It was just made with flour and rye on the back steps." It has had the same starter ever since. It was one of the first local bakeries to develop a real baguette, with a "dense, handmade quality" that is distinct from the "very sour" and "lighter" Boudin boule.

And about those baguettes.

"They're just beautiful. They're hand-rolled. That job of rolling baguettes is something we all love to do," Goldsmith shares. She talks about how "incredibly meditative" the process is, rolling hundreds of them, each one by hand, and how well it works in an industrial kitchen when there's space and time for everything in the rotation that managing sourdough requires—refreshing the starter, rolling the dough, enabling the rise and on. In this era when quickness is a virtue, Goldsmith says, "It's not something sourdough takes to. You have to slow down."

I am so inspired by her swooning poetic description of the subject that I will be quoting from her heavily here. On what sourdough really is: "Sourdough itself is a magic thing. It's the wild yeast in the air. You don't need Fleischman's. It's here, all around us. And it doesn't take anything to make it." Just flour, water, salt and "a leap of faith that it's going to rise and be this amazing thing."

Tartine sourdough, tender interior crumb. *Brandon Borrman.*

I learn from her that the process basically involves adding flour and water to flour and water, in rhythmic repetition, taking away and adding to, taking away and adding to, until you have a living, breathing little doughy wet mass that is capable of giving life to dozens, hundreds, thousands of loaves of beautiful bread—with a little care and feeding (of more flour and water) along the way.

Cheese Board over the years went from measuring things very loosely—using insider references to "pot-cheese buckets"—to now very precise recipes. But the influence of the environment and baker cannot be undersold. Goldsmith, again:

> It's just flour, water and salt. But even with a recipe, the flour changes, the temperature changes, the room changes. We're not doing it in a laboratory. There's an interaction you have with it. It's not like you close your eyes and you make it. You have to assess all the criteria, all the factors around you. If the weather's too warm, too cold, even the flours sometimes don't have the protein or the strength and you don't understand why it's so flat. And the salt is super important. If you don't put the salt in, you just get a sticky mass, it inhibits the growth of the yeast, the growth of the bread. So it is just flour, water and salt, but it's nuanced.
>
> It's science, and it's magic. And you can put your hands in it. It's an incredible, sensual, tactile experience. You hear it in the bowl, it's whacking, you're touching it....I really feel like everyone should—to make something, bake something from scratch—it's humbling, really.

Among the many bread bakeries following in the footsteps of Acme and the Cheese Board are Arizmendi (another bakery collective with a couple of locations in the East Bay and San Francisco); Della Fattoria (a not-to-be-missed café and bakeshop in Petaluma, with its own farm family of owner-operators and the best take on a sourdough one could imagine, featuring Meyer lemon and rosemary); and, in the early 2000s, Tartine.

Martha Stewart has shared his recipe, *Bon Appétit* (and a seeming one hundred other top media outlets) has covered his rise and San Franciscans have become maniacally devoted to his product. Chad Robertson is the old-school nouveau baker who made old-world bread on a small scale and took the city by storm.

Robertson and his wife, Elisabeth Prueitt, met in school at the Culinary Institute of America in Hyde Park, New York. After coming together and traveling the world—well, France and California—they started baking bread

On Starting a Sourdough Starter

The process of creating a starter, as Goldsmith describes it, is simple. Combine a cup of organic rye flour with a cup of water, and if you'd like, add a small piece of very ripe fruit (Cathy does not but acknowledges that some people do, "because there's yeast on the fruit") and leave the concoction on your counter.

Once it starts to ferment, you start to throw some away, keep a little, add more water and flour, let it grow a little more, throw some away, add more water and flour and onward and upward. Eventually, you should be replacing the rye with bread flour or whole wheat or whatever flour you'd like for the basis of your bread. She notes, "It gets more flavorful the more that you use it and change it and use it and change it."

"It's just an inoculation," she says, so you can start small. "Yeast is this thing: it's busy, it's busy, you feed it, it's tired, it's busy....You don't want an exhausted starter to begin with. You want to nourish new and young yeast cells to be growing." Takeaway: Start with a small starter and keep it that way as you grow, nourish and evolve it over the years.

and pastries for sale.[9] In 2002, after building a fan base at local farmers' markets, they opened Tartine—what *Bon Appétit* magazine now terms "the most influential bakery in America"—in the then-pre-gentrified Mission district of San Francisco.

French for "open-faced sandwich," the word *tartine* represents both literally and figuratively the bakery's concept. The shop does sell actual tartines, along with other sweet and savory dishes involving bread, but the word to me evokes a sense of containment, fulfillment, completeness. A sandwich—open-faced or not—is more than just its bread. It can be carried along with, enjoyed during a sit-down meal and tailored to all tastes. It is for everyone (like bread) but is also made or broken by the quality of the bread in which it's contained. And Tartine's bread is outstanding. Croissants are flaky and chewy at once, with golden-brown exteriors and a toothsome bite. And the sourdough's open crumb, tough and crisp exterior and wild yeasted tang represent the city's bread legacy in a gorgeous, modern way.

Exterior of Tartine Bakery in the Mission District of San Francisco, 2017. *Brandon Borrman.*

Entering the San Francisco bread scene almost a decade after Prueitt and Robertson was Josey Baker (real name), and he has since become a minor cult sensation in the bread-baking world. Two important facts: he only started really baking bread seven years ago (at age twenty-five-ish) and he mills his own flour.

Yep, bread in the city of San Francisco is that serious.

Baker is a Vermont native whose friend George gave him a sourdough starter seven (now likely eight, at the time of publication) years ago, and Baker "hasn't been able to stop since."

"Since that very first loaf, bread has played a crucial role for people," he says. "It's inherently a unifying thing; a loaf is meant for sharing, and in that it gives people the opportunity to come together. It also provides the baker with ample time for reflection and appreciation. From start to finish, bread just keeps giving!"

His enthusiasm is infectious via both e-mail and his bread. He opened a café/bakery in collaboration with Four Barrel Coffee, another local purveyor, in 2012, eventually deciding to mill his own flour in-house and dubbing the establishment The Mill. At the time, it was the only bakery in the city with its own stone mill to produce flour and use it for on-site baking.[10]

"I'm honored and humbled to be a part of the Bay Area food world," Baker says. "So much creativity and wisdom and dedication swirling around, it's hard to keep up with it all, but the nice thing is how inclusive it all is. It's really just one big family."

His most popular breads include dark mountain rye, country bread and something called adventure bread, which is just so perfect based on his seemingly exuberant personality. It's a gluten-free option, featuring all sorts of seeds (sunflower, sesame and flax), oats, almonds, almond flour and maple syrup.

Baker's primary source of distribution is direct to customer, through The Mill, but he also supplies bread to small markets in the area and select restaurants (including the James Beard Award–winning and Michelin-starred State Bird Provisions, as well as a personal favorite, Bull Valley Roadhouse, noted in the martini chapter, page 49). He is "surprised, excited, terrified and humbled" by his rocket-like success.

I asked him why sourdough is special. "Sourdough is the original bread. And looking back through time, most bread that humans have made has been sourdough. It wasn't until people started making yeast in laboratories and factories that there was anything else!" he exclaims. "Most people don't know this, but actually all of our bread is sourdough bread, meaning that it's all made with a wild yeast culture as the sole leavening agent. There's nothing sacred or dogmatic about it; I just believe that the most delicious and nutritious breads are made with a sourdough culture."

Moving from the new generation of bread makers back to an earlier stalwart who is still going strong, the Cheese Board's Cathy Goldsmith comments on the historic nature of sourdough and its juxtaposition with the city's sometimes full-court press toward the newest, latest trend. "I love the expanse of history…but am sometimes overwhelmed by how everything becomes hip or chic. There's a rush to have this next cool thing," Goldsmith reflects. "Bread is so important. It's a way to feed so many people. When it becomes Gourmet Ghetto [a reference to the several-block stretch of Berkeley that's become a modern foodie mecca], it's hard to be in touch with that sometimes. And I think it's important to be in touch with that."

Here's a way to be in touch with that in your own home kitchen.

Josey Baker's 100 Percent Whole Wheat
(notably with a sourdough starter)
Courtesy of Josey Baker, adapted from *Josey Baker Bread* (Chronicle Books, 2014)

Sourdough starter (*see recipe below)
Water
Whole-wheat flour
Sea salt, fine grind
Rice flour
Cornmeal (optional)

Special Tools
Proofing basket and cloth
Baking stone and oven-safe pot or bowl, or a Dutch oven
Large plate or pizza peel
Double-edged razor blade and handle

Gather your ingredients (Baker calls them "foodstuffs" in his book) and tools. Make your sourdough preferment 8 to 12 hours before you want to start mixing your dough—likely in the evening before you go to bed or in the morning. You want it to be the consistency of thick pancake batter. Put this stuff in a big bowl (for one loaf): 1 teaspoon sourdough starter (using a starter that is sour smelling in a good way, most likely between 12 and 24 hours old), ¼ cup cool water and ⅓ cup whole-wheat flour. Mix it up real good. Cover with a plate or plastic wrap and leave it alone for 8 to 12 hours.

Uncover the bowl and take a big whiff. It should be putting off a pretty strong smell, nice and yummy, maybe a touch sour. If it doesn't, no biggie; it'll still make awesome bread. Add 1½ cups lukewarm water, 3¼ cups whole-wheat flour and 2 teaspoons sea salt, fine grind. Stir it up with your strong hands until it's mixed together (30 seconds to a minute). Cover and let it sit for 30 minutes to an hour, whatever is convenient.

After it sits for a while, the dough is ready to be kneaded. Dip your hand in a bowl of water, then reach down into the side of the dough bowl, grab a little bit of it and pull it up and push it down on the top of the dough. Rotate the bowl a little bit and do it again. Be sweet and gentle yet firm with the dough. Do this to all of the dough; it'll probably take about ten folds. Cover the dough and let sit for ½ hour.

After ½ hour, stretch and fold the dough another ten times. Cover the dough and leave it alone for another ½ hour or so. Do this another two times, at 15- to 30-minute intervals.

Now you get to choose your own adventure for the bulk rise. Do what is convenient for you here. If you want to shape your loaf in 2 to 3 hours, let the dough sit out somewhere in your kitchen. If you want to shape your loaf anywhere from 12 to 48 hours later, stick it in the fridge (or just outside if it's cool out—about 45 degrees Fahrenheit).

After the dough has completed its bulk rise, flour your counter and dump out the dough. Pre-shape your loaf, then let it rest for 10 to 15 minutes. Shape it into a loaf and let it rest, seam-side down, while you line your proofing basket with a cloth that you've dusted with rice flour. Plop the loaf into the prepared proofing basket, seam-side up.

Choose your own adventure for the final rise. Again, do what is convenient. If you want to bake bread in 3 to 4 hours, let the loaf sit out somewhere in your kitchen. If you want to bake bread anywhere from 6 to 24 hours later, stick the loaf in the fridge (or just outside if it's cool out—about 45 degrees Fahrenheit).

Preheat. Put your baking stone or Dutch oven on the middle rack of your oven and preheat to 475 degrees Fahrenheit for 45 minutes.

Bake your bread. Sprinkle the loaf with cornmeal (or cover with parchment paper) and invert your loaf onto the large plate or pizza peel. (Or carefully plop the loaf into your preheated Dutch oven.) Slash the top with the razor, get it into the oven and cover it with a pot or bowl (or the Dutch oven lid). Bake for 20 minutes, uncover and get excited that your dough is magically turning into delicious bread. Bake for another 25 minutes. Check the bread and see how it's looking. If it's not dark brown, give it another 7 minutes.

Let it cool. Whole-wheat bread really benefits from a little rest before you slice into it. Because it's such a wet dough, it can actually have a slightly gummy texture if it's not given proper time to mellow out after its bake. So just be patient and give this loaf a couple of hours before tearing into it.

*Sourdough starter from Josey Baker
Mix and ignore: Mix together in an appropriate container with a lid ½ cup whole-wheat flour and ½ cup of cool water (60 degrees Fahrenheit). Stir it up real good with a spoon. You want it to be the consistency of thick pancake batter, so add a little more flour or water

if it needs it. But don't worry too much about it; exact measurements aren't important here. Loosely cover the container with its lid and let it sit for about 2 days at room temperature (60 to 70 degrees Fahrenheit).

After two days, compost most of the starter. Leave about a tablespoon's worth in the container.

Feed your starter. Pour in ½ cup of cool water. Use a spoon to stir and dissolve the starter that's left in the container. Add ½ cup of whole-wheat flour. Stir it up real good, loosely cover and ignore it for 2 days at room temperature.

Repeat. There'll be 2 weeks of this; every 2 or 3 days, compost most of your starter and mix in roughly equal parts whole-wheat flour and water. After 2 weeks, you'll have a healthy sourdough starter. Now go bake some bread.

Chapter 2

A CALIFORNIA ORIGINAL:
STEAM BEER, CRAFT BREWERIES

(Gold Rush)

On August 3, 2017, the news hit the airwaves: San Francisco's Anchor Brewing Company, originator of steam beer in 1896 and widely considered to be the pioneer of the craft brewing movement in America, had been sold. To "big beer." Big Japanese beer, to be specific: Sapporo.

My heart skipped a beat when I first heard the report on the radio. What would this mean for the city's most famous, most notably "independent" and most historically legendary brewery?

"When you take a brand like Anchor, its very soul exists in the heart of San Francisco," Keith Greggor, Anchor's president and CEO, told *SFGate* in an exclusive interview. "Of all the people we spoke to [about selling the business], [Sapporo] respected Anchor the most, what it stood for and the importance of its connection with San Francisco."

Greggor assured the media that nothing would change for the brew—not the recipe, not the brewing method, not the name. But I couldn't help feeling nervous. After writing about the experience of touring the brewery and distillery (Anchor also makes a great old-fashioned genever-style gin and whiskey on-site, though this part of the business will now be separate) in my last book, my non-beer-drinking self had been converted. I'd fallen for Anchor Steam—the most widely known of the company's beers, so much so that many people mistakenly call the company itself "Anchor Steam." I wondered if the tasting room experience would remain the same, focused on not only the steam beer but also Anchor's lesser-known and oftentimes truly exclusive brews, not available in retail outlets, or if instead it would be diversified by Sapporo's products, little gold stars popping up on the shelves behind the tasting counter, the establishment gradually, silently morphing into more of an international-anytown bar rather than a San Francisco original. At least in age, the two companies seem compatible peers; Sapporo claims to be the oldest beer company in Japan, given its 1876 birthdate.

Without a crystal ball, it's hard to say what Anchor's future looks like. But at this point, it remains a steadfast city treasure—available in most every bar across the town's seven- by seven-mile spread, beckoning residents and tourists alike to imbibe a taste of gray sunshine, a taste of the city's foggy rooftops and miraculously gorgeous vistas on a clear day.

Anchor historian and packaging design manager Dave Burkhart recounts how it all started for the beer "that is like no other in the world." Like so many other culinary origin stories for San Francisco, its *steam* moniker is hard to nail down. Note, though, the trademark: the official term "steam beer" is unique to Anchor.

"Anchor Steam® Beer derives its unusual name from the nineteenth century, when steam seems to have been a nickname for beer brewed on the West Coast of America under primitive conditions and without ice," Burkhart explains. But the specifics of the nickname's derivation have several possibilities, he says. "Steam" could be a reference to the steam that rose from the hot wort—the unfermented ground malt infusion that provides the basis for beer—as it cooled on the city's rooftops in shallow, open pans, he explains. Or it could be a reference to "the pressure of natural carbonation developing in the kegs," or a third option: a reference to "the foamy 'head of steam' that spilled over the top of each glass."

It all started back during the California Gold Rush, in the late 1840s, when the region was a fervent magnet for dream-seekers and becoming flush with newly wealthy miners, with all of the cultural, society-establishing activity that went with a burgeoning population. This included the influx of lots of immigrants as well—by 1850, about a quarter of the state's population was foreign born[11]—Germans among them. Burkhart shares their role in Anchor's history:

> During the California Gold Rush, German brewers—including Anchor's first brewmaster, Gottlieb Brekle—sought to make the lager beers that were so popular in the mid-nineteenth century. Lagers (from the German, meaning to store) are made with lager yeast, which thrives at very cold temperatures. Without ice or modern refrigeration, brewers improvised, taking advantage of the temperate climate to cool and ferment their "lagers"

Anchor Brewery, Russian Hill, back in the day. *Anchor Brewing Company.*

in shallow, open pans. These temperatures, closer to typical ale than typical lager temperatures, created different flavors and aromas. The beer was then kräusened[12] *and delivered to saloons around town. When tapped, the kegs often emitted a hiss and spray like a steam engine—one of the theories about the origins of the nickname "steam beer."*

No one else can call their brew "steam beer"; the term is trademarked by Anchor. And the modern Anchor Steam still carries flavors of its original, at least to some extent.

"Anchor's brewing traditions have been passed down from brewmaster to brewmaster for over 145 years," Burkhart explained. "The resultant beers today are unique: a sum of their parts and a sum of their history, coupled with modern methods of sanitation and quality control."

That history reflected in today's beer goes roughly as follows: in 1871, Brekle bought an old saloon on Pacific Street near Russian Hill for $3,500 and turned it into a brewery. In 1896, another couple of German brewers— Ernst F. Baruth and his son-in-law, Otto Schinkel Jr.—bought Brekle's brewery and named it Anchor, presumably for its connection to the city's port status. Ten years later, Baruth died, the brewery burned down in the fire after the great earthquake and then, just as it was being rebuilt in a different location, Schinkel died too. More German brewers fortunately came into the picture and kept Anchor going…for a few years anyway. Until Prohibition hit. From the 1920s through the early '30s, there's no official record of Anchor doing business. After restarting in 1933, it experienced another fire, more stops and starts and a stop again in 1959 when mass-produced beer temporarily killed Anchor's business. In 1965, Fritz Maytag swooped in, a young Stanford grad keen on keeping his favorite beer alive, so the story goes. A few years later, he was bottling the beer for the first time and started a few other small, rather "micro," lines, and thus began the era of craft brewing in the United States.

Bottom line on Anchor Steam: it's light, bright and of its place. It has a taste of triumph and decades of German traditions married with Californian sensibility—a taste of renewal. It's a unique taste of San Francisco and should be enjoyed in its environs, alongside a bowl of rich soup (perhaps a chowder at Boudin or an utterly addictive, downright perfect seasonal soup at the Westin St. Francis Hotel in Union Square; ask chef Thomas Rimpel for the Dungeness crab chowder with Anchor Steam and muenster). Kick your heels up, pondering the origins of the steam name and the staying power of a proper city rooftop brew.

Pro tip: Not to be missed, not so much for beer drinkers but cocktail enthusiasts, is the distilling arm of Anchor, formed in 1993. It makes its own rye whiskey and gin, including a delightful Old Tom Gin that is perfect in a Martinez.

Chapter 3

HANGTOWN FRY: ARE THOSE BIVALVES IN MY EGGS? AKA MAN'S LAST MEAL

(Gold Rush)

B oth delicate culinary gems suspended within shells, connected to earth's foundational elements of land and water, eggs and oysters find favor together in a famous local dish that is really perfect for any meal of the day. The stars of the show were expensive ingredients back in the heady days of the California Gold Rush, when the northern foothills seemed dusted with mid-nineteenth-century magic and dreams became reality for many young men. And it was in this context—we think—that the Hangtown Fry, essentially a fried oyster omelet, was born.

Like so many of the region's culinary legends, the Hangtown Fry carries with it an element of dispute—and disrepute, for that matter. Its origin story is hard to nail down but has been commonly associated with the modern town of Placerville, dubbed Hangtown in its early days for the way in which it punished criminals: by hanging them from an old oak tree in the center of town.

Placerville is located not far from the site of the discovery that started it all—where James Marshall found flakes of gold in the river as he worked to erect Captain John Sutter's sawmill in Coloma—and eventually became a supply center for camps in the mining region. Not surprisingly, the town saw its population swell with wannabe miners traveling through the area to try to get a piece of the action. A town full of aspiring or newly rich people naturally meant some level of show-offiness, and what better way to show off than to demand expensive foods? So goes one common origin story anyway, that a newly flush miner wandered into a local eatery—believed to be the saloon of the El Dorado Hotel (today's Cary House Hotel now sits on the site)—and asked for the most expensive dish available, and a cook met his needs with a scramble of eggs, oysters and bacon. Culinary historian Erica Peters notes that there was an "18-carat hash" on the menu, and while neither eggs nor oysters appeared on that bill of fare, an egg may have been mixed into the pricey hash to justify the name. She also reports that it was St. Francis Hotel chef Victor Hirtzler who gave the dish a name, in print, in 1919. His Hangtown Fry called for mixing "one dozen small, fried California oysters" into plain scrambled eggs.

Just three years later, the following quote from the April 13, 1922 edition of the *Sacramento Union* showed how the dish still captured imaginations even seventy years after its rumored birthdate:

What did they eat in the days of '49? Can you recall any of the favorite dishes of the gold rush days and how to prepare them? The Sacramento Union *is anxious to print series of short, snappy recipes of popular '49 dishes. Ask your grandfather or grandmother to describe their favorite early day dish. Send your recipe to the* Sacramento Union *and it will be printed with your name as the contributor, here's starter. Do you know what Hangtown fry is and how it is prepared? The Hangtown fry was one of the choicest of '49 dishes.*

In the twenty-first century, the Hangtown Fry remains a dish on most classic menus in the San Francisco area and has made appearances on numerous hot new tables. In the latter department, celebrity chef Tyler Florence featured it on his early menus at the ever-delicious, comfort food–focused Wayfare Tavern, a restaurant that tips its hat to the city's culinary history in a pubby space while pulling in hypermodern crowds for lunch and dinner. Apropos of this book, it should be noted that Wayfare even includes this quote from Clarence Edwords's seminal work on the San Francisco culinary scene, *Bohemian San Francisco: The Elegant Art of Dining* (1914), on its website: "This aggregation of cuisinaire…a most wonderful variety of food products in highest state of excellence, has made San Francisco the Mecca for lovers of gustatory delights, and this is why the name of San Francisco is known wherever men and women sit at a table." Florence has also regularly featured takes on the city's famous green goddess salad, updated with delicate butter lettuce and shaved radishes.

Brenda's French Soul Food, a "new" classic joint (established in 2007 and recipient of much acclaim over its first decade in business), offers a

Wayfare Tavern's open kitchen on a Friday night, 2017. *Brandon Borrman.*

straightforward take on the dish. It is absolutely addictive doused with the Crystal hot sauce at the ready throughout the place and served with a hearty, unctuous helping of creamy, cheesy grits—the best I've ever had—and a beautiful, fluffy cream biscuit. Local publication *SF Weekly* named it the "Best Hangtown Fry" in the city in 2014. Nestled between the still gritty Tenderloin and European majesty of the Civic Center area downtown, the establishment is like a magnet for "cool," its customers a diverse mix of bearded and tattooed thirtysomethings dining alongside young families, government employees and multigenerational gatherings of women (at least on my last visit), with the backdrop of massive cement walls sporting gracefully threatening cracks that seem to beckon to another world. Brenda's also features a dish I've never seen anywhere else: a flight of beignets, filled with alternately sweet (chocolate or Granny Smith apple) and savory (crawfish with cheese and cayenne) fillings. Go with a crowd and order as many things on the menu as you can.

Longtime personal favorite, and purportedly the oldest restaurant west of the Mississippi, Tadich Grill also offers a popular, conventional rendition of the dish—because really, when you go to Tadich, you're not looking for molecular gastronomy or new takes on anything. Waiter David on a recent

Tadich Grill, 2017. *Brandon Borrman.*

Friday night told me the dish is his wife's favorite. He said, "We always have it as an appetizer," which I actually did that night as well. Not your typical light starter—as it's quite filling—it was the perfect prelude to the house cioppino (also a favorite, see chapter six).

The recipe I'll include here is the traditional take from another favorite classic restaurant, one that's all about keeping things steady, reliable and as-has-always-been-done: Sam's Grill. (Look to chapter twelve for the establishment's version of Celery Victor, an utterly weird-good salad, to use that term incredibly loosely.) I include Sam's version of the Hangtown Fry not only because it's good but also because it's representative of the restaurant's roots: original owner Sam Zenovich was a seafood man. In an undated news article from sometime in midcentury, kept informally in the restaurant's "archives," the author lists a series of seafood specialties on offer at Sam's, writing, "All prepared as they were 'in the old days' when eating was an art and people took more time to indulge in the necessary pastime than many do today." So indulge in the following recipe at home, and be sure to take your time with it.

Sam's Grill's Hangtown Fry
Serves 2

6 large eggs
½ cup milk
1 cup bread crumbs (sourdough bread preferred)
3 tablespoons butter, divided
4 ounces Olympia oysters (shucked)
4 strips bacon
½ cup all-purpose flour

Beat 2 eggs in a bowl with ½ cup milk to be used as egg wash. Place bread crumbs in a shallow dish. Melt 2 tablespoons butter in a double boiler and skim off the top of the butter after it has melted. Beat the remaining 4 eggs in a bowl. Strain the oysters. Fry the bacon crisp.

Dredge the oysters in flour and then place in the egg wash. Roll the oysters in the bread crumbs. Fry the oysters quickly in a frying pan with the melted butter (1 to 2 minutes). In a small Teflon-coated frying pan, melt 1 tablespoon butter and place the beaten eggs in the pan. Cook for about 1 minute over medium heat and then add the oysters. Cook for about 1 more minute and then flip the eggs and oysters over and cook until done. Place the bacon on top and serve.

Chapter 4

BEHOLD, THE MAJESTY OF THE MARTINI—AND ITS DELIGHTFUL, LESSER-KNOWN PREDECESSOR, SORT OF, THE MARTINEZ

(Gold Rush)

S tudying the history of San Francisco's original foods and drinks is not as clear-cut as one might think. Tall tales and proud claims weave together into a fabric of murkiness, where it's impossible to discern the colorful, distinct threads used to create the textile, as the end result is one ruddy mass.

Collecting stories from aficionados and historians on the subject is an exercise in persistence, patience and discipline. It's also about acceptance that the "real story" may be not be ultimately discerned definitively and may instead be an amalgam of them all. Acclaimed cocktail historian David Wondrich articulates this conundrum expertly when it comes to the martini in his seminal book, *Imbibe!*:

> *We may never know the true origin of the King of all Cocktails. It's possible that a definitive answer lies entombed in the crumbling pages of an old newspaper somewhere, waiting for some lucky researcher to stumble upon it, but it's equally possible that the first meeting of gin and vermouth was one of those momentous occasions that don't seem all that momentous at the time; that everybody involved took their drinks, smacked their lips, and toddled on home without further remarking the occasion....What early evidence we have is hazy and contradictory, and as always, that has allowed a number of theories to bloom.*

The theories are so hazy, so variantly believable and so prolific that Wondrich devoted an entire appendix in his book to meting them out. The mythology and its relative attributions can be categorized into three basic buckets: New York, San Francisco and the neighboring city of Martinez. For the purposes of a book devoted to San Francisco's legacy foods, I give a bit more weight to the Bay Area theories, but that is founded mostly in my regional bias. (That said, I'd argue that that tendency is common when it comes to the subject everywhere it is discussed.)

Why do we care so much, you might ask? Because. The. Martini. Is. Awesome. A perfect drink. Straightforward. All about the liquor and the environs in which it's being consumed. Leah Bhabha said it well in Food52:

> *The martini, with its basic ingredients and air of refined panache, is one drink that cannot be outshone by the latest trends. From James Bond's widely recognized "shaken not stirred" endorsement to Ernest Hemingway's pronouncement in* A Farewell to Arms, *"I've never tasted anything so cool and clean....They make me feel civilized," this gin-based beverage has been and will continue to be an iconic stalwart of the cocktail lexicon.*[13]

Word, sister. Hemingway captures exactly what *I* love about a martini: it makes me feel civilized. It smooths the edges on a rough day and immediately makes me feel fancier than I am—even if I'm already wearing pajamas and have just put my kids to bed. Researching for this book the drink's heavily researched and disputed origins became a maddening exercise—until I would pause and swiftly stir up a martini, sip slowly and think about the beauty of the drink itself. (My preferred composition and method: 2¼ ounces Sipsmith gin, ¼ ounce extra-dry La Quintinye Vermouth Royal, stirred at least 100 times in a mixing glass full of ice, strained into a glass with a single pimento-stuffed martini olive, which I don't eat, but instead give to my husband after I've finished my drink.)

Bhabha neatly encapsulates some of those stories in her piece, sharing how author and martini expert Barnaby Conrad III "claims that the drink was, in fact, invented in San Francisco, after a miner requested a pick-me-up in the city on his way to Martinez."

She continues: "There are also assertions that it originated in New York's Knickerbocker Hotel. Still others assert that the drink was named after 'Martini & Rossi' vermouth, which was first created in the mid-1800s. Apparently in the interest of brevity, the drink became known as the 'Martini.'"

It is the Martinez story that will be my focus here, as it sounded the most sensible, based on Pony Express routes, what I imagine about gold miners,

Carter Wilson, martini aficionado and researcher, in the bar of Sunflower Garden restaurant, near the alleged site of the birthplace of the martini, Martinez, California, 2017. *Brandon Borrman.*

the location of the town itself and one key character: Carter Wilson. When the name was suggested as a top resource on the history of the martini, the referrer enthused, "He's got binders and binders full of research. You've got to talk to him." This was after someone else told me said referrer was "my guy" on the subject.

Hopeful I wasn't diving down a rabbit hole, I wrote to Wilson. We met two days later at a Chinese restaurant in Martinez, in San Francisco's East Bay region. The town's case for being the martini's birthplace is arguably strong—strong enough that in 1992, it erected a monument to it, and isn't that the mark of indisputable proof?

Tucked into a back booth, my recording devices scattered across the table alongside his famous binders, we introduced ourselves to each other; he promptly ordered a martini. He knew the owner, Sandy, by name, and efficiently handed our server a card. "That's my order." The card detailed precisely how he likes his martini (4 parts vodka, ½ part dry vermouth, lemon peel, olives, drops of chartreuse), a creation by his daughter, sweetly still in her hand, years ago.

Wilson's love of the classic drink began when he was fairly wee and was charged with making his father's nightly martini as a child. A Prohibition-era bathtub gin producer, his father was an absolute connoisseur of the drink. But there was one problem. "He would also fall asleep at the dinner table," Wilson recounted. "I thought it was the juniper berries." He tested the theory one night by using vodka instead of the classic gin, and his dad never nodded off tableside again.

It was these early experiences that paved the way for Wilson's love of the martini (including his choice of vodka rather than gin) and his interest in its origins. That, along with his reverence for his chosen hometown as an adult, Martinez, and his membership in a gold rush–era fraternal organization called E. Clampus Vitus (or the Clampers for short), devoted to partying and philanthropizing on behalf of "widows and orphans" (part of their original mission), alongside honoring and documenting some of history's lesser-known milestones. They've put up plaques all over the Bay Area marking historical moments, and once you know this, you'll start noticing them throughout San Francisco and beyond.

After much digging through local papers and historical archives (hence the binder), Wilson subscribes to the Martinez theory of origin, outlined on the plaque that his chapter of the Clampers erected in town to mark the cocktail's birthplace. So reads the plaque that emblazons a stout, rocky monument situated in the corner of an otherwise unassuming parking lot in town:

> *On This Site in 1874, Julio Richelieu, Bartender, Served Up the First Martini When a Miner Came into His Saloon with a Fistful of Nuggets and Asked for Something Special. He Was Served a "Martinez Special." After Three or Four Drinks, However, the "Z" Would Get Very Much in the Way. The Drink Consisted of 2/3 Gin, 1/3 Vermouth, a Dash of Orange Bitters, Poured over Crushed Ice and Served with an Olive. Humorist James Thurber Once Said "One Is Alright, Two Is Too Many, and Three Is Not Enough."*

There is even a full-sized martini inside the monument—one that remained intact in 2017 when a car collided with the historic marker, ripping off the rocky top. (There's no sign of the incident today, given Wilson and his fellow Clampers' swift repairs.)

What is interesting about Wilson's theory is that it even splits the city's origin story further—claiming that the long popular belief that Richelieu's bar once stood on the spot where now-defunct watering hole Amato's proudly served the locals was not quite true; it was, in fact, down the street and around the corner. This dispute caused minor controversy with the Amato family, you can imagine, as they'd passionately represented the theory on radio talk shows and to newspapers on many occasions. But Wilson found historical evidence that demonstrated the contrary, including the testimonials of Annie Olsen, age ninety-three in 1992, who had lived across the street from the site of the moment in what was formerly her parents' house. She quoted her father as having said there was an old saloon across the street through the twentieth century. This theory was corroborated by former president of the Martinez Historical Society Charlene Perry, who found tax records that proved there was a saloon on the corner of Smith and Thompson Streets (today, Alhambra

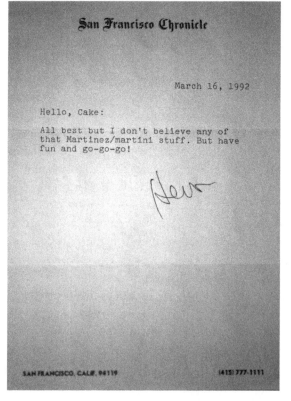

San Francisco Chronicle

March 16, 1992

Hello, Cake:

All best but I don't believe any of
that Martinez/martini stuff. But have
fun and go-go-go!

SAN FRANCISCO, CALIF. 94119   (415) 777-1111

Above: Monument to the birthplace of the martini in Martinez, California. *Brandon Borrman.*

Left: Letter from the famed *San Francisco Chronicle* columnist Herb Caen to "Cake," pal of Carter Wilson, on the martini mythology. *Carter Wilson's collection.*

and Masonic Streets, the site of Wilson's monument) in 1874, along with an 1890 photograph showing a saloon in that spot.

Central to Wilson's research is the word of former fire chief and town historian John "Toddy" Briones, brother-in-law to Julio Richelieu. It was Briones who, in 1964, testified that Richelieu invented the cocktail in 1874 for a gold miner customer who was "looking for something to drink that would keep him warm on his ferry boat trip to San Francisco." So Richelieu made him a "Martinez Special," consisting of three parts Old Tom gin, one part French vermouth and a dash of orange bitters, poured over ice and topped with an olive.

One of the most jovial people I've met, Wilson was never deterred by his detractors, instead endeavoring to welcome them into the Martinez camp fold. He even proudly invited local columnist and San Francisco theory proponent Herb Caen to the plaque dedication, receiving correspondence about the event that he treasures even today.

Wilson disputes the San Francisco theories with logic and research. "It just doesn't make sense that a bartender would name a drink for where a customer is going; they'd name it for their own place, their own city." He says that Richelieu did move around, at one point operating a bar in San Francisco as well at Third and Market—but notably after his time in Martinez. The Occidental Hotel, workplace of famous bartender Jerry Thomas through the 1800s—and other claimant of the origin story—was right up the street, Wilson notes. He points out that Thomas's 1862 bartending book does not include a recipe for the Martinez cocktail and that the drink was only later added to an edition of the 1887 guide. The Court of Historical Review, a mock court presided over by real judges that rules over passionately disputed cultural matters, sided with the San Francisco theory in 1983, only to have the "ruling" reversed by the Martinez Appellate Court, which sided with the Martinez origin story.

But where did the maraschino—the element that seems to distinguish a modern "Martinez" cocktail from a martini—come in?

Emma Janzen of *Imbibe Magazine* aptly describes what we find called the Martinez cocktail on (rare) modern menus as a "velvety blend" of Old Tom gin, maraschino liqueur, sweet vermouth and bitters.[14] Even after asking quite a few bartending experts and historians about the presence of maraschino in the martini drink and how it got there, I came up short. It is the bartender's prerogative to add an element here or there to make his own drink, and from what I can determine, that explains the martinez-martini-martinez conundrum, too. Someone along the way decided to add maraschino, and it

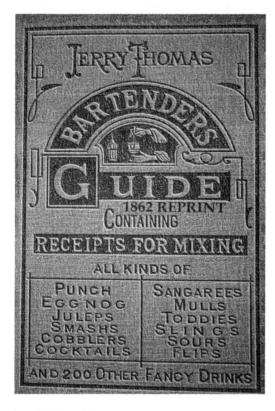

Left: Cover of reprint of Jerry Thomas's *Bartenders Guide* from 1862. *Brandon Borrman.*

Below: Recipes for martini and Martinez cocktails as they appear in Trader Vic's *Bartender's Guide*, 1947. *Brandon Borrman.*

MARTINEZ COCKTAIL

¾ oz. gin   ½ tsp. orange bitters
¾ oz. French vermouth   ½ tsp. curaçao
  Stir with cracked ice; strain into chilled cocktail glass.

MARTINI COCKTAIL—DRY

1 oz. dry gin   ½ oz. French vermouth
  Stir with cracked ice; strain into well-chilled cocktail glass.
Serve with stuffed olive. Variation: For a not so dry Martini,
use equal parts gin and French vermouth.

stuck with the Martinez theory in a more lasting way. So I share some of the many iterations of the two (or more?) drinks here.

Tiki drink legend "Trader Vic" Bergeron provides this maraschino-less recipe in his *Bartender's Guide* from 1947:

¾ ounce gin
¾ ounce French vermouth
½ teaspoon orange bitters
½ teaspoon curacao

Stir with cracked ice; strain into chilled cocktail glass.

Use of the curacao, a common ingredient in many tiki drinks, makes sense, and its proximity to maraschino liqueur—while lacking the nuttiness—is close in resemblant sweetness.

Bergeron's recipe for a straightforward martini (which he lists as "Martini Cocktail—Dry") takes a two-to-one ratio of gin to vermouth:

1 ounce dry gin
½ ounce French vermouth

Stir with cracked ice; strain into well-chilled cocktail glass. Serve with stuffed olive.

Variation: For a not so dry Martini, use equal parts gin and French vermouth.

In William "Cocktail Bill" Boothby's accounting of the method in his *How to Mix Drinks* book (1908), the martini cocktail sounds a lot like the modern Martinez:

Martini Cocktail, No. 27

This popular appetizer is made without sweetening of any description, as the Old Tom Cordial gin and the Italian vermouth of which it is composed are sweet enough. Into a small mixing-glass place a piece of ice, four drops of Angostura bitters, half a jigger of Old Tom Cordial gin, half of a jigger of Italian vermouth and a piece of twisted lemon peel; stir thoroughly, strain into a small bar glass and serve with ice water.

Side note: pre-Prohibition-era cocktails often seemed to be served with ice water on the side. My father, an ice water obsessive—the glass must be absolutely full of ice first before adding the water—though born long after the Volstead Act was lifted, would likely appreciate this fact.

Bartender Stanley Sliter pouring Palace Hotel manager A.H. Price the first drink at the Happy Valley bar, the first to open under a new state law at the time that allowed sale of liquor by the glass, San Francisco, 1934. *San Francisco History Center, San Francisco Public Library.*

Today, you can obviously get a martini almost anywhere that serves hard liquor, but there are a few places in San Francisco I'd highly recommend for the experience. Alleyway supper club Bix serves a delicate version, diminutive in size and light in effect, but the Art Deco atmosphere and other-era sensibility is hard to beat. Capitalizing on the Art Deco vibe is Stookey's Club Moderne in Nob Hill, a neat little lounge that highlights classic cocktails, features a "cocktail of the month" program and has a little "city favorites" section on the menu that spotlights the mai tai, Irish coffee and pisco punch. Both are sweet little distinctive spots and capture a bygone era of cocktailing, but they are not, in fact, my favorite martini purveyors. My three go-to spots for martinis in the city are Tadich Grill, Sam's Grill and Zam Zam.

Tadich and Sam's are pseudo-siblings: unrelated in ownership but absolute kindred spirits, they are the kind of places you think of when you fantasize about the three-martini lunch.

Tadich is the oldest restaurant on the West Coast and one of the oldest in the country and feels it in the best way. Wait staff is mostly of a certain generation, mostly male and have mostly worked at Tadich; they hail from a time when waiting tables was a respectable, lifelong profession. They know their jobs well and make no fuss about anything; wishy-washy orders are not really tolerated, but advice is given if requested. And the bartenders make a fantastic classic martini—ice cold, with options of traditional and craft gins (or vodkas, if you don't like flavor), procurable while you wait in the long line along the wall for your table.

Sam's is similar, a favorite of local dignitaries, power players and introverted writers like me, and though it was founded as an oyster stall in 1867, the team has done a brilliant job of keeping pace with the times. They opened a patio aimed at happy hour specials and drawing the growing population of downtown millennials in the Financial District to a very old restaurant. A church-like glow remains in the lovely dining room, where you'll spot cut lemons awaiting in bowls on the tables and hat hooks on the walls, all a superb environment for enjoying expertly prepared seafood, their specialty. The best place for a martini at Sam's is tucked away in one of the secret, curtained booths adjacent to the main space, and that martini will be exactly to your liking: cold, gin-based and dry, with either a twist or olives, depending on how you order it.

In the Haight, a neighborhood best known for being the epicenter of the hippie movement and home to the Grateful Dead house (I used to live right across the street!), Persian-themed Zam Zam looks like a movie set, with its gracious semicircular bar and a cinematic backdrop of a gorgeous, colorful mural, but acts like a regular neighborhood bar. Its famed former proprietor, Bruno Mooshei, was notorious for his surliness and intolerance of subpar orders, but his martini became legendary: Boord's (a London dry gin) and a whisper of dry vermouth (allegedly at a ratio of 1,000 to 1). And the thing is gigantic—supposedly just three ounces, but I swear it feels like six. The late, great San Francisco columnist Herb Caen dubbed the place "the Holy Shrine of the Dry Martini." I highly recommend a moment of worship there.

The best place to enjoy a true "Martinez" cocktail—or a martini in the style of the original described by Boothby—sits outside the city limits, near the town of Martinez, in the tiny, somewhat desolate old waterfront town of Port Costa. Stepping inside the Bull Valley Roadhouse feels like stepping into a saloon from the late nineteenth century and immediately brings vibrant life to what feels like a ghost town. Bull Valley even shares a short menu of pre-Prohibition cocktails with online visitors, and in-house, guests can read said menus through an old-timey magnifying glass to offset the low lighting in the bar. It proves its expertise in this realm to modern bar visitors with precisely made drinks that take one back to a time before their own.

Tamir Ben-Shalom is the Albany native and brilliant beverage director who spent time at Acme, Pizzaiolo and the Slanted Door before joining the Bull Valley team and helping develop the authentic cocktail menus. He divulged an occupational hazard in the bar business today: a martini doesn't mean the same thing to all people. They know no boundaries or city limits, so everyone thinks they know what a martini is, but there is not a shared language or mind-set between the masses for what makes a martini.

"It's always tough to decipher the martini from the guest to the server to the bartender; so here's what we give our servers," he said, sharing with me the two-page document that provides a bit of history and a hilariously biting assessment of what people know or do not know about the martini today, used as an in-house coaching tool. While there isn't room to reprint the entire document here—and boy, I wish I could! it's a gem—here are some highlights.

"Martini cocktail" on Bull Valley Roadhouse pre-Prohibition menu, viewed through a house old-timey magnifying glass, 2017. *Brandon Borrman.*

It says "of the famous cocktail, it is probably one of two explanations," and what follows is this straightforward description:

1) Naming drinks before 1890 wasn't very creative and usually explained the drink clearly. "Martini Rossi" was the Italian vermouth of choice back then. Using equal parts of Martini Rossi and gin would probably give the name Martini because the Italian vermouth was the dominant flavor. It also can sell because "Martini Rossi" was the name brand. Sell a "martini cocktail" and you are selling the Jack Daniel's part of a jack and coke. Well…kind of.

2) On the west coast, we like to say it's from our sexy city of Martinez. It would make a lot of sense too. The cocktails are very similar and the Martinez cocktail is simply an original martini with maraschino. The name is very close, but that's as far as we can go with that. Now it's hard to tell which cocktail came first. They were both printed in numerous books during the same time period. So which cocktail evolved into which hasn't been proven. I would lean towards no. 1, but don't tell anyone from around here that.

Ah! Tamir! Sacrilege! You are representing the region but choosing a wholly different origin story! Shocking, to say the least. But I do love where he goes with the explanation: "There is no right or wrong with the martini. It's simply about getting that boozy drink in a drinkers' hands the way they think they want it. How that is, is a big game of telephone."

He proceeds to include a play-by-play mock script for what he typically experiences with guests ordering martinis, which, among other hilarious moments, disparages lemon drops and honors the concept of guests' wishes. Here's a snip:

Tamir: What would you like to drink?
Guest: A Martini!!
Tamir: Hmm…gin or vodka?
Guest: Vodka
Tamir: We have Spirit Works and two potato vodkas to choose from
Guest: I'll just take the well
Tamir: Ok. Would you like an olive or a twist
Guest: Olive
Tamir: Would you like it served up or over (on the rocks)?

Guest: Up
Tamir: Great
Guest: Wait! Wait! Make it very, very dry
Tamir: Ok. Should I use vermouth at all?
Guest: no vermouth, thanks.

Done. Now I have served vodka up with an olive. The most important part of the conversation is the amount of vermouth. My experience tells me that once they say "very dry," you must get in there and find out if they want it or not. They might believe vermouth is the devil. Beware! They are ready to send that drink back even if the bartender hasn't touched the vermouth bottle all night.

The guide continues with the house's understanding of definitions and recipes—from dry to very dry and more—and feels like a secret window into an insider's world of modern bartending at a place that honors the craft and its history. From the Churchillian—the former UK prime minister famously said the only way to make a martini was with ice-cold gin and a bow in the direction of France—to the historic hybrid with both sweet vermouth (Italian) and bitters, Bull Valley is the place I'd go for the spectrum of the martini experience. Bar experts will make you a gin-based sup with a whiff of vermouth, if you so choose, or a lemon drop (UH, NOT A MARTINI), or a beautiful, rich, subtly sweet Martinez cocktail. Tamir and his team are good. And you can imagine movers and shakers of yesteryear sipping stiff coolness, feeling elegant and in the know, while you caress an old magnifying glass and nibble Josey Baker bread with sea-salt butter or Tomales Bay mussels, steamed and perfect, alongside your cocktail, feeling both of the old and the new and local all at once. Cheers to you.

Martini Cocktail from Bull Valley's Pre-Prohibition-Era Menu

Half a mixing-glass full fine ice, three dashes orange bitters, one-half jigger Tom gin, one-half jigger Italian vermouth, a piece of lemon-peel. Mix, strain into cocktail-glass. Add a maraschino cherry, if desired by customer.[15]

Chapter 5

CHINESE-AMERICAN SPECIALTY: CHOP SUEY

(Gold Rush)

Circa 2017. On a short little Chinatown street strung with red lanterns and twinkling lights, itself a vision ready for the silver screen, sits the most modern Chinese restaurant I've ever dined at. In just its first year of business (2016), it earned a Michelin star, along with much acclaim for chef Brandon Jew and his team, which includes his wife, Anna Chet-Lee Jew, a designer, decorator, hostess and "eye" extraordinaire. Their restaurant, Mister Jiu's, shares a block with a "fashion shop," a "florist and aquarium" and a hair stylist named Deanna—all daytime businesses that make for one sleepy nighttime stretch. At night, the street is deserted, seemingly lifeless, all its shops dark behind locked gates pulled down to the sidewalk.

All but one, of course: Mister Jiu's, the restaurant where seemingly everyone goes, presumably Ubering or walking from other parts of the city, as there's nowhere to park easily in Chinatown but for the Portsmouth Square Garage (which seems to be a secret only Chinese visitors to the neighborhood know about).

Cartoony vertical font makes up the restaurant's black-and-white sign out front—a sign, I feel compelled to add, that appropriately includes the possessive comma in the restaurant name. I mention this fact because I so appreciate it, as it's a feat that seems potentially challenging given the sign's vertical construct, easy to overlook, and it indicates a reverence for appropriate grammar that often seems lacking in this emoji- and acronym-heavy texting culture of today. Seeing it makes me like and trust the Jiu's team—the Jews—and believe in their attention to detail.

Mister Jiu's, Chinatown, 2017. *Brandon Borrman.*

San Francisco Chinatown postcard, twentieth century. *Lauren Thor.*

My work on the book took me to this Michelin-starred restaurant darling, a haven for the young, hip and monied of San Francisco, as it's what Chinese food can mean in the twenty-first century. Its connection to this book lies in its locale: it occupies the space formerly devoted—for decades—to two of the most famous Chinese restaurants in the city. Most recently, it was the Four Seas, a classic family banquet house where Jew himself spent many meals, "peeling red-dyed boiled eggs and slurping down longevity noodles," according to one report.[16] Before that, it was home for years to one of the most famous chop suey palaces of the city, Hang Far Low.

On my first visit, I kept saying, "This is good...really, really good," throughout the meal. I was charmed by the drinks and swift service, the glowing fish tanks built into the back bar, the generous and warmly lit dining room—designed by Chet-Lee—and a dish (roast quail with a creamy, pork-studded house-made sticky rice, from their fall menu) that I want to eat for the rest of my life. Need. Need to eat for the rest of my life. It was comforting and warm, full of indistinguishable bits of delicious meat and felt like a homey amalgam of all the casseroles of my childhood, minus the cheese.

I imagine this may have been what the people who ate chop suey in San Francisco in the late midcentury—and that's mid-nineteenth century, not twentieth—must have thought, though in a less indulgent, privileged way, when they first tasted it. This likely would have been the white gold miners, it's important to note, not the Cantonese residents who reportedly ate a familiar home-cooked dish in the same neighborhood before the miners were introduced to it. Food, science and technology writer Peter Smith recounts in his article for *Smithsonian* magazine[17] a historical reporting of some expectant and demanding miners coming into Macao and Woosung, a Chinese buffet-style restaurant in San Francisco, considered one of the first, if not the first, Chinese restaurants in America, wanting food at closing time. Smith quotes a 1937 *Harper's* article by Carl Crow that tells the tale of the owner quickly making do by gathering all the leftovers "his Chinese patrons had left in their bowls, put[ting] a dash of Chinese sauce on top and serv[ing] it to his unwelcome guests," telling them in Cantonese they were eating "chop suey, or 'beggar hash.'"

Smith writes of the dish as maintaining "a reputation for being the biggest culinary joke ever played; the butt-end of which were American diners, too stupid to know they were eating what has been variously translated as 'mixed bits,' 'odds and ends,' or 'garbage.'" But both Smith and Erica Peters, in her culinary biography of San Francisco, refer to Andrew Coe's *Chop Suey: A Cultural History of Chinese Food in the United States* for the story that preceded the tale of a vengeful restaurateur. Peters explains:

> *Chop suey (*shap sui *in Cantonese) was initially a stir-fry of various vegetables and organ meats. The dish was brought to America by Chinese from the Sze Yap area, just to the south of Guangzhou. These Cantonese arrived on the West Coast, but by the 1880s many had continued on to New York City.*

Peters explains that the name of the dish appears as "chop soly" in several regional articles in the New York area in the late 1880s but that "non-Chinese San Franciscans did not start appreciating chop suey until around 1900." And in 1904, "a San Francisco cook, Lem Sen, showed up in New York claiming to have invented chop suey and demanding royalties from all East Coast restaurants advertising the dish. He failed in that effort, but succeeded in highlighting San Francisco's attachment to chop suey."

1915 "Chop Suey—Chinese" from the *Pan-Pacific Cook Book*[18]

Barely cover a small chicken with water and boil until tender; then shred the meat, return the bones to the soup, boil down to one cup; then strain. Cut a half pound of lean pork into thin inch strips and fry; when brown, add the chicken, a half cup of celery, cut thin, a small piece of chopped onion, six dried Chinese mushrooms (which have soaked in water), six water chestnuts, cut thin, a quarter of a pound of wheat or bean sprouts, half a chopped green pepper, and a small piece of ginger-root, crushed. Pour over all the chicken broth and season well with very little salt and a tablespoon each of gu yow and soy sauces to be found in any Chinese provision house. Simmer for a few minutes and serve with rice.

Back in 2017, young chef Jew's enthusiasm was infectious during our conversation about his remake of the old chop suey–cum–banquet house, a childhood home of his that he felt "deserved another life."

"It was an important restaurant in the community for a long time," Jew explains. "People celebrated important parts of their lives here." But in recent years, the neighborhood had in large part morphed into one that caters to tourists, Jew said. "It was a historic neighborhood that wasn't really being recognized by locals anymore." He wanted to bring back, at least in a small way, its glory days of local revelry and celebration. "A place that has the unique feel of Chinatown, while showing the contemporary side of the Bay Area. Pay homage to the past but keep pushing contemporary ideas as well."

On chop suey, Jew has been pondering the dish. "The hardest thing about chop suey is that it's been a kitchen sink kind of recipe. I can't really find an end-all-be-all, tried-and-true, historic chop suey. There are so many versions, so many different combinations. Even with that understanding, trying to come up with our own version, I haven't really figured out yet. But I have the desire because of the historic context in the neighborhood."

His earnestness is obvious as he talks about the building's "great soul" and uncovering hidden treasures like gold leaf and black writing that spells out "100 ways to write prosperity" in the upstairs former banquet room, which he and his team are also reviving. Not renovating or remodeling, he specifies, but restoring. "What's actually here is amazing." Jew reveres the "golden era of Chinatown" and marvels at how his restaurant was once one that could fit seven hundred people across its three floors. And you can see him working

Chinese in the City

Chinese food in San Francisco began with, as many things did, the gold rush—with an influx of Chinese immigrants fleeing "poverty and harsh conditions in southern China" in the mid-nineteenth century. That population surged in the 1860s with recruitment for work on the railroads, leading to a sizeable community in the Bay Area that set up other businesses (like restaurants). But what those restaurants served evolved over the decades, starting from southern Chinese home-cook dishes (like chop suey) to Chinese-American foods and phenomena (including the Chinese takeout craze, starting with Johnny Kan's Chinese Kitchen in the 1940s); followed by Cecilia Chiang's game-changing establishment of the Mandarin restaurant in 1968, the first presentation of spicy Szechwan and Hunan cuisine in the United States; and in an elegant dining environment; to, now, Brandon Jew.

People dining at Hang Far Low chop suey restaurant on Grant Avenue in Chinatown, February 9, 1946. *San Francisco History Center, San Francisco Public Library.*

through his own heritage as the accolades collect and Mister Jiu's firmly takes shape. He shares:

For me, Mister Jiu's is also about defining my identity as a Chinese American. When we first opened, there were dishes that made it seem like three or four different restaurants here—dishes that were very traditional, dishes that were not very traditional, dishes that were very Californian. For

Open kitchen at Mister Jiu's, Chinatown, 2017. *Brandon Borrman.*

me, it was about finding out what was right. I was trying to get comfortable in my identity as a Chinese American.

That's how I've felt most of my life, really. Being able to cook it out and express it has been really fun to see. What I've observed is everyone has a different context to Chinese cuisine, especially in America. There are certain parts of America where the only Chinese food you can get is at a mall. Or at a mom and pop.

Nothing like a fancy restaurant that attracts both the city's youth and affluent elite, like Mister Jiu's does. Jew talks about how he's bringing what he learned at other revered San Francisco restaurants such as Zuni and Quince—and their focus on seasonality and small farm-sourced, organic ingredients—to the concept of Chinese food, what it is and what it can be, as seen through the lens of a millennial Chinese American chef who grew up in the Bay Area.

"Trying to translate the actual flavors" in Chinese dishes using California-sourced ingredients "has been a really fun puzzle for me to figure out. Like, how do we use avocados? How do we use artichokes? How do I use those products to translate what a Chinese chef's mentality would be?"

Jew also wants to influence what local farmers grow and expand their repertoire into more traditional "Chinese" ingredients. His grandfather, whose house he still lives in today, is no longer alive but saw Jew open the restaurant that bears the family name.

If Mister Jiu's is a taste of San Francisco Chinese food in the twenty-first century, Sam Wo is its previous century predecessor. A culinary institution that claims to be the oldest restaurant in Chinatown—from its initial opening in 1907 "by three immigrant siblings from Taishan, China"[19] after the big earthquake—Sam Wo reopened, revitalized, in 2015, after a health code–related shutdown threatened its existence. Today, the famed former late-night haunt of beat poets (Allen Ginsberg purportedly dined there after his reading of *Howl* at City Lights in 1955) and other city notables still feels like a dive but is now a registered national landmark and relatively clean and features young wait staff (some of them family) and a social media–friendly photo screen out front for visitors to create digital postcards of their visit.

While food-wise the restaurant is best known for its *jook* (a traditional porridge, which is absolutely delicious) and noodle soups, I was there for the chop suey, naturally. Though it's not one of their most famous dishes, I found it to be one of the tastiest things on the table—as did my young

The rear of Mister Jiu's kitchen in Chinatown, nighttime, 2017. *Brandon Borrman.*

children, who relished eating piece by piece the green beans and broccoli florets sautéed with delicate bean sprouts in garlic and onion. "There are so many different versions of chop suey," said a server. "Depends on where your family is from. My family is from the south, and this is what I remember from my childhood." I was fascinated to discover the dish in the vegetable section of the menu, as it contained no noodles, meat or rice. It was certainly homey and simple—one I could imagine on home tables any weeknight.

General manager Julie Ho, daughter of former employee and eventual owner David Ho, describes the nothingness of the dish she grew up with when I asked her how Sam Wo's compares to others':

> As a little girl, I didn't think much of the dish and just thought the name itself sounded funny in English (in Cantonese it was simply "stir-fried mixed vegetable"). Going out to other restaurants, I haven't encountered much of any chop sueys or really noticed it. On the rare occasions that we did go out to a restaurant to eat, it was one of Dad's rules that we do not order anything that we can make ourselves at home or at the restaurant, especially one as simple as the chop suey.
>
> It's really a mixture of whatever excess vegetables [are around], stir-fried into a convenient dish. Each time it is made, it may be slightly different than the other times it was made. Chop suey is an old-school name, and I really do appreciate it when someone uses that to order the dish.

Ho reflects on her journey from child of the restaurant, through server and kitchen prep staff, and now to management:

> Growing up at the old Sam Wo, I have never really given much thought about what an institution the restaurant was. Sure, customers have come in and shared with me their excitement of going to the restaurant and made a big deal; to me, it was just a part of my childhood and adult life. The restaurant represented family, craziness, new experiences—a place which I learned as an adult was quite unordinary for the Regular Joe.
>
> To this very day, it just feels like a way of life. It's nothing extraordinary, just a place where we can curb cravings and bring back old memories or even sprout new memories. Seeing those customers making new discoveries, those enjoying themselves and those reminiscing, makes me feel that [taking on the restaurant] was well worth it.

Left: Reflections of Chinatown and photographer in front window of Sam Wo restaurant, 2017. *Brandon Borrman.*

Right: Kids like Sam Wo's chop suey, 2017. *Brandon Borrman.*

Chop Suey, as described by Julie Ho of Sam Wo

When asked about the recipe for chop suey, my father simply says, "Grab handfuls of whatever vegetables that are closest to you; prep the wok with ginger, garlic and a little oil after the wok is 'red' (hot); throw in the random vegetables; add a heavy pinch of salt; stir it a few times; when the wok is nice and hot again, throw in a spoonful of water for hydration; stir it a couple times again; then scoop it up to the plate."

And whether it's the pan you use or the nonchalance you apply to the method, the final result can be extraordinary.

Chapter 6

AN EMBARRASSMENT OF FISHERMEN'S RICHES: CIOPPINO

(late 1800s)

Rich, but not fatty rich. Subtly sweet, but a touch too sweet and it's nasty. Soupy enough to mop up the extra broth with a hunk of dense sourdough bread, but not watery. Deeply tomatoey, absolutely not creamy and loaded with local seafood. This is cioppino, the iconic Italian fisherman's stew that has become synonymous with the concept of traditional San Francisco cuisine. All the classic old restaurants worth their salt in town have a version, as do a number of modern establishments. And for something that is essentially a tomato stew with seafood in it, the variations and subtleties across the cioppino landscape raise winners into the ethereal culinary clouds and leave lesser attempts in the dust. Several of these will be covered in this essay. But first, let's honor history.

Cioppino is said to have entered San Francisco's environs by way of the Italians in the late 1800s, most likely on fishing boats. *Ciuppin* was the name given to a Genoese fish stew Italian fishermen would throw together with the day's catch. Erica Peters uncovered a story by reporter and future aviator Harriet Quimby, who had spent a day with Italian fishermen in 1901, returning to write about the "chespini," which she describes as follows in the *San Francisco Call* of October 6, 1901:

> *This is the way to make it. My authority is a scrap of soiled paper written in Italian. Translated, it says: "Put into kettle half glass of sweet oil, one clove of garlic, two large tomatoes, two chili peppers, one glass of white wine; prepare fresh fish, cut in small squares, drop into the sauce and cook three minutes; serve hot." It really tastes much better than it sounds.*

Italian fishermen at Fisherman's Wharf, North Beach, 1912. *California History Room, California State Library, Sacramento, California.*

I asked Peters about the "sweet oil" mentioned in Quimby's description and what that could possibly be beyond olive oil. Like a good historian, she dug further, unearthing a variety of sources, which she put together to assess that yes, it must have been olive oil. My favorite was this one, for its matter-of-fact, definitive nature, from the *Bulletin of the North Carolina Department of Agriculture* (1915), which reads, "Any oil other than olive oil branded sweet oil would be misbranded. It is not correct to label cotton-seed oil sweet oil." Okay, then!

Published the same year as that bulletin was *The Pan-Pacific Cook Book,* including its own take on ciuppin/chespini/cioppino, here:

Ciopino Neapolitan

Chop two onions and half a clove of garlic fine, with two branches of parsley and a stick of celery, and fry until yellow in a half a cup of olive oil; add a can of tomatoes and a cup of white wine and boil for half

LA's Don the Beachcomber vintage menu. *California Historical Society.*

Palace Hotel crab salad (with green goddess dressing in background). *Palace Hotel.*

Palace Hotel green goddess dressing. *Palace Hotel.*

Right: Fritz Maytag, former owner of Anchor Brewing Company, home of Anchor Steam beer. *Anchor Brewing Company.*

Below: Vintage postcard showing Trader Vic's San Francisco. *Lauren Thor.*

Vintage menu from Bernstein's Fish Grotto, San Francisco, California. *Author collection.*

Right: Vintage menu from New Joe's restaurant, San Francisco, California. *Author collection*.

Below: Vintage postcard showing San Francisco Chinatown's iconic Grant Avenue. *Lauren Thor*.

Grant Avenue, Chinatown

Vintage postcard showing Cliff House, San Francisco. *Lauren Thor.*

Wayfare Tavern's green goddess salad with butter lettuce, 2017. *Brandon Borrman.*

Left: Sam Wo restaurant, Chinatown, San Francisco, 2017. *Brandon Borrman.*

Right: Chop suey at Sam Wo, Chinatown, San Francisco, 2017. *Brandon Borrman.*

Sourdough bread from Tartine Bakery, 2017. *Brandon Borrman.*

Left: The famous Mission burrito from La Cumbre Taqueria, 2017. *Brandon Borrman.*

Below: Burrito fans through the ages show their love on an antique guitar at La Cumbre Taqueria. *Brandon Borrman.*

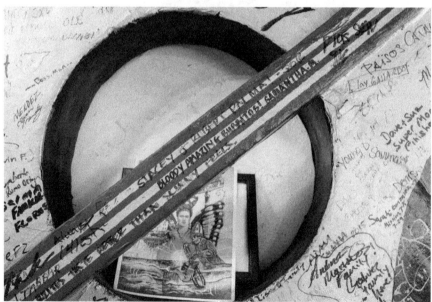

Left: Mai tai in a proper vintage vessel at Leo's Oyster House, 2017. *Brandon Borrman.*

Right: Martini aficionado and builder of historic plaques Carter Wilson enjoys his drink of choice at the Sunflower Garden restaurant in Martinez, California. *Brandon Borrman.*

San Francisco's Chinatown at night, with Mister Jiu's, 2017. *Brandon Borrman.*

Left: A Boothby cocktail at Cockscomb, San Francisco, 2017. *Brandon Borrman.*

Right: Classic and pre-Prohibition-era cocktails, including the martini cocktail, at the Bull Valley Roadhouse, Port Costa, California, 2017. *Brandon Borrman.*

The temple of the martini, Aub Zam Zam, Haight District, San Francisco, California, 2017. *Brandon Borrman.*

The Celery Victor, accompanied by a proper martini, at Sam's Grill, 2017. *Brandon Borrman.*

Deep red leather booths beckon guests to the dining room at Original Joe's in North Beach, San Francisco, 2017. *Brandon Borrman.*

Afternoon crowd at Trader Vic's in Emeryville, 2017. *Author photograph.*

An indulgent Hangtown Fry, with side of grits and a biscuit, at Brenda's French Soul Food, San Francisco, 2017. *Author photograph.*

Gorgeous Irish coffees at the Buena Vista Café, 2015. *Brandon Borrman.*

Copper kettles at Anchor Brewing Company, San Francisco, 2015. *Brandon Borrman.*

Left: Holiday crowd at Buena Vista Café, 2017. *Brandon Borrman.*

Below: Taps in the tasting room at Anchor Brewing Company, 2015. *Brandon Borrman.*

Beloved official ice cream sandwich of the city, San Francisco's It's It, 2017. *Brandon Borrman.*

an hour; add two pounds of fish, cut into large portions (using several kinds), half a pound of scrubbed clams or mussels and a boiled crab (with outside shell removed), broken into pieces. Season highly with salt and paprika and simmer until the fish are done. Pour over toasted French bread in a large, deep platter.[20]

I love the touch of serving this dish directly on top of French bread (and note it says "French" and not "sourdough," relevant for the emergence of the sour aspect of bread in the city around the same time) and the fact that the crafty creators of the *Pan-Pacific Cook Book* advise using a platter. For soup. I can see it now, long platters lining elegant buffet tables at the Pan-Pacific Exposition itself…filled with toasty bread soaking up ladlefuls of bright red, rich fish soup.

Inquiring about which seafood restaurant in Fisherman's Wharf today is the real originator—or the best purveyor—of the popular stew goes nowhere good, simply because this is a glorious dish, and who wants to fight over who made it first in a restaurant? Nevertheless…

Alioto's founder, Sicilian immigrant Nunzio Alioto, started his fish stall in 1925 and was serving seafood cocktails and crab out of it just a

Vintage menu from Sabella and La Torre, Fisherman's Wharf classic since 1927. Features a city classic, crab cioppino, as well as its "out of the shell" sibling, the bouillabaisse. *Brandon Borrman.*

few years later, in the early '30s. When he died, his wife, Rose, took over and expanded the business, eventually opening a real restaurant in 1938, becoming purportedly the first woman to work on the wharf and one of the first to sell the seafood stew. (This is "Nonna Rose's Famous Crab Cioppino" on the menu today and tastes just what you'd imagine an Italian grandmother's specialty stew would taste like—awesome. Don't confuse it, though, with the "Sicilian Seafood Stew" also on the menu; the latter is bouillabaisse, French in heritage, with a base of fish stock and white wine, plus a few tomatoes but less tomatoey than the cioppino, with the addition of saffron and more vegetables. Also awesome, though.)

Part of the next generation of wharf hot spots was Scoma's, founded about thirty years after Alioto's in 1965 by Al Scoma and his brother Joe when they bought a little coffee shop that had been serving breakfast to local fishermen. Today, Scoma's offers one of my favorite versions of cioppino—in addition to keeping its swinging '60s vibe alive in the backdrop of a newly remodeled and updated front of the house. Theirs is the Lazy Man's Cioppino, so named for the fact that all the work has been done for you—shellfish de-shelled, seafood neat and tidy in the bowl, mostly submerged in deep, red broth, sourdough on the side, with a thick cloth napkin for cleanup.

Back to the '30s, a peer of Alioto's is-slash-was Fishermen's Grotto No. 9, founded in 1935 by another Sicilian immigrant, Michael Geraldi. The

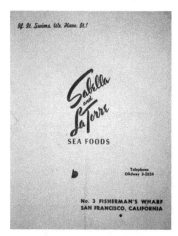

Front of vintage menu from Sabella and La Torre restaurant reads: "If it swims, we have it!" *Brandon Borrman.*

restaurant was an utter favorite of my childhood for its many themed dining rooms and perfect shrimp and crab cocktails. And sourdough bread! And, duh, cioppino! And crab Louis! I heart SF! The restaurant was the first full-service, sit-down restaurant when it opened. After eighty years of family management, the Geraldis put it up for sale for nearly $6 million; fortunately, Chris Henry, a local restaurateur who appreciates a good vintage business, took it on. Henry has other legacy San Francisco businesses to his name (including the hofbrau-style Tommy's Joynt) and has updated the restaurant "gently," as local food writer Marcia "Tablehopper" Gagliardi puts it,[21] reopening the iconic crab stand out front, massaging dining spaces and the menu. Now, you can get the famous crab cioppino with the option of making it lazy, for a little extra money.

Post-2000, there's been a proliferation of restaurants that serve cioppino. One is even named after the dish, with some celebrity chefs in its fanbase. And then there are others, like Sotto Mare.

We arrived to a wait. A long one. We clutched our incredible crab-shaped vibrating buzzer, shivered outside, laughed and waited for our cioppino. It was me, my husband, Brandon, and our best friends Cori and Michael, who walked up to the bar as we waited.

"I'll have what you're pouring," Michael told the barman. Or the dude sharing wine with happy people nearby (he wasn't sure).

"Whatever I'm pouring?" the man repeated. "Red or white?"

"Red," my friend said.

Pause. Man of the house pours. Hands friend glass.

"What do I…? Owe? Do I pay at the table?" Michael says.

Man: "Tonight's your lucky night. You drew the lucky number. Salud."

Friend walks back outside to us in disbelief. Excitement. We later realize the "man" is the owner.

This is Sotto Mare: familial, Italian, popular and with a feeling that is old and long-standing. Sotto Mare's walls are covered in paraphernalia and photographs, lining the narrow bowling lane of a space, with crowds out the door and a wait staff that's surly but sweet. Although it's been a food business going back to the mid-twentieth century, the restaurant itself was founded after the millennium. On the menu, Benita's Baccala is a brilliant starter—traditional salt cod mixed with tomato and studded with capers and presented in the shape of a fish (of course)—and the menu is full of seafood classics (oysters, cocktails, louis, chowder and pasta dishes). The "best damn crab cioppino," as advertised on the menu, is not, in my book, the best (sorry! I know, Michael Bauer would disagree with me…). The dish looks beautiful, absolutely full of crab; however, the penne filling the bottom of the bowl leaves me wanting and slightly confused. Pasta in cioppino? I'd never seen it before. And the tomato broth is just a touch too sweet for my taste.

The judgment is probably not fair, though, seeing as how Tadich Grill will forever have my heart in the cioppino department. The establishment is the oldest, the most old-man-dominant in the server department, the most San-Francisco-at-its-start—and the house cioppino is just utterly unadulterated tomato-and-seafood pleasure, presented in a cozy half booth, with a very cold martini alongside. (You can also get the Hangtown Fry as a starter here, which seems insane but is a brilliant move.)

So I'd go to Alioto's and Scoma's for the atmospheric wharf experience (including killer views); to Sotto Mare to feel like part of the family (and that baccala); and to Tadich for the cioppino. It is just so damn good. Bib offered and always worn proudly. And if I'm feeling in the mood for a chefy take on the classic, I'd make Michael Mina's mother-in-law's version, which appeared in *Food & Wine* magazine in 2005. The best thing about this recipe (as expressed by modern master Mina) is that it doesn't deviate but rather honors the classic dish.

Judith's Dungeness Crab Cioppino, courtesy of Michael Mina

Renowned modern chef Michael Mina's eponymous and acclaimed San Francisco restaurant has spawned a growing restaurant empire around the world. He has shared a recipe for cioppino, made traditionally on Christmas Eve by his late mother-in-law, Judith Tirado.[22] It appears here with his permission.

¾ cup extra-virgin olive oil
8 large garlic cloves—6 finely chopped, 2 whole
3 jalapeños, seeded and minced
2 red bell peppers, finely chopped
1 large onion, finely chopped
1 large bay leaf
2 tablespoons tomato paste
½ cup dry red wine
1 28-ounce can peeled tomatoes, finely chopped, juices reserved
4 8-ounce bottles clam broth
1 ½ cups water
Salt and freshly ground pepper
½ cup packed basil leaves
½ teaspoon crushed red pepper
4 steamed Dungeness crabs, about 2 pounds each (see note)
2 dozen littleneck clams, scrubbed
2 pounds firm, white-fleshed fish fillets such as halibut, skinned and cut into 1 ½-inch chunks
2 pounds large shrimp, shelled and deveined
2 pounds mussels, scrubbed
1 pound sea scallops, halved vertically if large
Crusty bread, for serving

Tadich Grill cioppino, 2017. *Brandon Borrman.*

Step 1: In a very large soup pot, heat ¼ cup of the olive oil until shimmering. Add the chopped garlic, jalapeños, bell peppers, onion and bay leaf and cook, stirring occasionally, over moderately high heat until softened and beginning to brown, about 10 minutes. Add the tomato paste and cook, stirring, for 1 minute. Add the wine and cook until nearly evaporated, about 1 minute longer. Add the chopped tomatoes and their juices and cook over moderately high heat until slightly thickened, about 5 minutes. Add the clam broth and water, season lightly with salt and generously with pepper and bring to a boil. Simmer over moderate heat until the broth is reduced to about 8 cups, about 20 minutes.

Step 2: Meanwhile, in a mini food processor, combine the basil leaves with the whole garlic and process until the garlic is finely chopped. Add the remaining ½ cup of olive oil and the crushed red pepper and process the basil purée until smooth. Season with salt and pepper.

Step 3: Working over the sink, pull off the flap on the undersides of the crabs. Remove the top shells and discard. Pry out the brownish insides and pull off the feathery lungs and discard. Rinse the crab bodies in cold water and quarter them so that each piece has body and leg.

Step 4: Add the crabs and clams to the pot. Cover and cook over high heat, stirring occasionally, until the clams begin to open, about 5 minutes. Using tongs, transfer the crabs to a large platter. Add the fish, shrimp, mussels and scallops to the pot, pushing them into the broth. Return the crabs to the pot, cover and cook, stirring occasionally, until the clams and mussels are fully open and the fish, shrimp and scallops are cooked through, about 8 minutes longer.

Step 5: Ladle the cioppino into deep bowls and drizzle each serving with some of the basil purée. Serve with crusty bread and pass the remaining basil purée separately.

Make Ahead: The Dungeness crab cioppino can be prepared through Step 1 and refrigerated for up to 3 days.
Tip: Have the fishmonger steam the crabs for you.

Chapter 7

FORTUNE COOKIES: NOT WHAT YOU THINK THEY ARE

(late 1800s)

I think I'd be hard pressed to find a person in the United States who hasn't seen or eaten or at least heard of a fortune cookie. Certainly there'd be a few people, but not many. We all seem to know the little treat, its accessible sweetness and the fun and mystery it presents with each initial cracking open of the folded, crisped dough. But the cookie that comes after every meal in a Chinese restaurant or stuffed into a bag of Chinese takeout boxes is not what you think it is. It's not actually Chinese. Its roots are in Japan, and in this country, its birthplace (or rather place of introduction to America)—or so I will say as part of a book on Bay Area classics—is San Francisco.

An amateur historian and lifelong medical photographer figures prominently in the research of the fortune cookie's Californian heritage. His name is Gary Ono, and he gave San Francisco a culinary gift: extensive family research on the origins of the cookie. In 1906, his grandfather Suyeichi Okamura founded Benkyodo, a little Japanese confectionery and snack shop that ultimately became a temple of mochi and manju artisanry. It remains one of the oldest businesses in the city's Japantown, but not many people know that it is purportedly one of the first, if not the first, American mass-producers of the fortune cookie.

Though Ono, who spent ages three to five in a Japanese internment camp with his family during World War II, remembers his family making fortune cookies after the war at the shop when he was a child, his curiosity about his family's connection to the cookie's origins was piqued during the 1970s as the movement for reparations to those who had spent time

Benkyodo Candy Factory storefront, with owners, including Suyeichi Okamura (*second from left*), circa 1906. *Gary Ono.*

Visitors have tea and cookies in the Japanese Tea Garden in Golden Gate Park, 1941. *San Francisco History Center, San Francisco Public Library.*

in camps surged. He began research in earnest on Japanese American and his own family history, which led to his documentary about his father's role as a wartime radio broadcaster, called *Calling Tokyo*. He began interviewing family members and following the trail of the stories until a full picture emerged: In the early twentieth century, Benkyodo took over the production of fortune cookies for the Japanese Tea Garden in San Francisco's Golden Gate Park for Makoto Hagiwara, a Japanese immigrant who founded the building of the tea garden—and they have the same *katas* (fortune cookie molds) to prove it.

Los Angeles lays claim to the cookie's U.S. origins as well, and Ono has interviewed members of the family that owned the prominent Japanese bakery there as part of his research (they actually know Ono's relatives). The debate between the two cities about the origin story reached such a fever pitch that in 1983, San Francisco held a mock trial to resolve the claim once and for all.

New York Times writer Jennifer Lee has done extensive research on the cookie—including interviewing Ono—and documents her findings in her book *Fortune Cookie Chronicles*. In a *New York Times* article in 2008, she addresses the dispute about the history:

> *The cookie's path is relatively easy to trace back to World War II. At that time they were a regional specialty, served in California Chinese restaurants, where they were known as "fortune tea cakes." There, according to later interviews with fortune cookie makers, they were encountered by military personnel on the way back from the Pacific Theater. When these veterans returned home, they would ask their local Chinese restaurants why they didn't serve fortune cookies as the San Francisco restaurants did....But prior to World War II, the history is murky.*

Ono introduced Lee to Yasuko Nakamachi, a Kanagawa University grad student who discovered a nineteenth-century book of stories and illustrations from Japan that shows the existence of the cookie there first. It makes sense that a Japanese immigrant to America (Hagiwara) around the same time would bring with him the tradition—and the *katas*. She remarks in the same *Times* article:

> *A character in one of the tales is an apprentice in a senbei store. In Japan, the cookies are called, variously,* tsujiura senbei *("fortune crackers"),* omikuji senbei *("written fortune crackers"), and* suzu senbei *("bell crackers"). The apprentice appears to be grilling wafers in black irons over coals, the same way they are made in Hogyokudo and other present-day bakeries.*

Lee goes on to discuss Benkyodo's role as well as that of the bakeries down south:

> *A few Los Angeles–based businesses also made fortune cookies in the same era: Fugetsudo, a family bakery that has operated in* [Little Tokyo, Los Angeles] *for over a century, except during World War II; Umeya, one of the earliest mass-producers of fortune cookies in Southern California, and the Hong Kong Noodle company, a Chinese-owned business. Fugetsudo and Benkyodo both have* [used] *"kata" black iron grills, almost identical to the ones that are used today in the Kyoto bakery.*

Benkyodo Candy Factory interior, purported birthplace of the fortune cookie in America, early 1900s. *Gary Ono.*

Ono adds that Benkyodo was given the bulk of the Japanese Tea Garden's *kata* to produce a greater volume of fortune cookies.

Today, the cookies are no longer made by Benkyodo; the shop is fairly devoted to its stunning mochi and manju, leaving no room physically in the space for the giant old *kata* machine.

"My son Tom actually has a jar full of fortunes," Ono tells me when I share my secret OCD-style obsession: saving the paper fortune from nearly every fortune cookie I eat.

Today, Ono volunteers for the Japanese American National Museum in the Little Tokyo neighborhood of Los Angeles. And he does, on occasion, eat fortune cookies: "I don't go out of my way to buy bags of them, but I do enjoy a cookie at a restaurant."

Ono not only represents the story of the fortune cookie in San Francisco; he's also an example of how interconnected and tightly woven the histories of San Francisco residents and neighborhoods can be. Japantown is nowhere near Chinatown, but the city itself is intimate. Merely crossing a street can take you from a fancy neighborhood to a gritty one or from one ethnically historic spot to another.

Ono's connection today to the Chinese treat with Japanese roots is one that's come full circle from his first job in photography: as a nineteen-year-old student at San Francisco City College, he worked as a backstage film developer and printer at the famous Forbidden City nightclub in Chinatown. "A girl with a camera would walk around to the tables, taking pictures, and then shuttle the film to me behind the stage. I'd process it in time for the customers to take home a souvenir picture of their time at the club."

Local reporter Gary Kamiya captured the era in an *SFGate* article on January 9, 2015:

> *Starting in the late 1930s, San Francisco's Chinatown unexpectedly exploded as a jumping nightlife destination. Clubs like the Chinese Sky Room, the Kubla Khan, the Lion's Den, the Dragon's Lair, the Club Shanghai, and the most famous joint of them all, the Forbidden City, attracted throngs of whites and Chinese alike with their all-Chinese floor shows—scantily clad chorus girls and dancers, comedians and singers. These nightclubs flourished for close to 25 years, providing a jolt of glamour, sexiness and show business panache to traditionally conservative Chinatown.*[23]

The way that Ono's path led from helping out at his Japanese family's bakery (which happened to be the first fortune cookie maker in the city, and allegedly United States), to an internment camp, to photographing the city's elite at Chinese nightclubs is remarkable to me, as it seems to signify the cultural commitment and cultural bleed we experience in the Bay Area. Distinct communities bringing their traditions to others and an overlapping and layering of traditions into new identities. A world of cultural precision and fusion at once.

The best place in San Francisco today to see fortune cookies made is, naturally, in Chinatown, at the Golden Gate Fortune Cookie Factory. A narrow, industrial space that looks unchanged from its 1962 founding, the factory is tucked away on a little alley in the neighborhood, just up from Portsmouth Square, a one-block park full of people playing board games, doing tai chi or pausing to navigate next steps in Chinatown. The cookie-making temple welcomes visitors and still does things the old-fashioned way, by hand. Several women sit next to antique cookie presses, deftly pulling off the freshly pressed disks of dough, shaping and stuffing them with fortunes individually. It's an awesome spot to take kids, though it's standing room only; the folks at the factory are generous with samples that are literally hot-off-the-presses, and taking home bagfuls is not an expensive endeavor. On our last visit, their generosity with samples kept our young children (ages three and four at the time) entertained for blocks afterward, crunching their little cookie rounds (samples are unformed) and pleading for more as we made our way down the steep hill to have chop suey for lunch.

Chapter 8

JACK-OF-ALL-TRADES:
BILL BOOTHBY AND HIS NAMESAKE COCKTAIL

(1891–1908)

"San Francisco has the best bartenders in the U.S.," John Burton told me matter-of-factly. As the California chairman of the United States Bartenders Guild, he should know. A lifelong barman, he's known thousands of his kind over his long career in the business.

Now in his late seventies, Burton has become a force on the national bartending scene, starting work as a professional bartender in 1959 and over the years becoming an educator, consultant, author, subject matter expert and collector—and a pleasant guy to chat with, to boot. Or to booth. (Sorry, couldn't help myself.) He knows an inordinate amount about bar history, including the life and times of William T. "Cocktail Bill" Boothby and his namesake cocktail.

"He was a San Francisco legend," he explained. "A state assemblyman, a minstrel, in the real estate business, a barman—a jack-of-all-trades. He knew a little about everything but not a helluva lot about anything."

Boothby was most famously a bartender at the Palace Hotel, purported originator of some other of the city's famous culinary marvels. But he also served behind the bar at myriad other establishments, first allegedly in other big U.S. cities, such as New York, Philadelphia and Chicago, and then at a number of places in the Bay Area, including the Parker House, Byron Hot Springs (a bygone resort situated east of San Francisco in Contra Costa County that once catered to the rich and famous in the early twentieth century)[24] and Hotel Rafael Club House in Marin County. And he certainly seemed to believe in himself and his special talents in the industry. In the introduction to his lauded bartending guide *The World's Drinks and How to Mix Them* (1908), he sets the stage for his reader about the legitimacy of the book right up front with this wonderful quote:

> *Many pamphlets heretofore written upon the theme of mixology are absolutely worthless, owing to the fact that they have been gotten up in the interest of some cheap publishing house which has paid some celebrated mixologist a royalty for the use of his name only, while some inexperienced, unprincipled individual is the real author. These so-called guides contain recipes for the mixing of beverages which no practical bartender on earth ever had occasion to serve. The only redeeming features of these decoctions are their high-sounding names, which scheming, imaginative penny-a-liners have given them in order to make large volumes out of little material.*
>
> *I have neither asked nor received assistance of any description in the compilation of this book, the hints, suggestions, recipes and commandments being the fruit which my own individual tree of experience has borne. Therefore, I can challenge the world to ridicule or disprove anything herein contained.*

Palace Hotel Court postcard, date unknown. *Lauren Thor.*

The work wasn't Boothby's first foray into writing about his craft. His *Cocktail Boothby's American Bar-Tender* (1891) was published nearly two decades earlier when he was just a wee thing in the bartending world; he'd only been in the industry a few years when he turned twenty-nine. Cocktail historian David Wondrich says the content of the book wasn't unique at the time.

> [But] *when he published a second edition, in 1900, he had another decade of mixology (plus running a restaurant, ticket-scalping and no doubt a dozen other hustles) under his belt. He had also earned the right to be known as The Honorable William T. Boothby, having served a year in the state legislature.*

Wondrich is a revered writer for good reason: his eloquence and lilting rhythm of words always paints a precise picture of bygone subjects. I love what he says about the profession of bartending back in the day:

> *Back during the long First Golden Age of the cocktail, between the end of the Civil War and the beginning of Prohibition, bartending was a respected profession, if not necessarily a respectable one. That is to say, if you were successful at it, you wouldn't win any civic awards, and church ladies would sniff when you walked by, but regular working men would consider you to be a figure of substance, a pillar of the neighborhood. This meant that many professional barmen set out to be just that, apprenticing at an early age, climbing their way up from barback to bartender to head bartender to saloonkeeper.* [25]

And he goes on, taking up the subject of the moment—Bill Boothby:

> *Others, however, took a more crooked path. Take William Thomas Boothby, the San Francisco bartender who was, in the years before Prohibition, the dean of West Coast mixologists. Born in the city to Forty-Niner parents in 1862, Boothby proved himself at a young age to have a great deal of that useful quality, hustle. Among his early occupations were vaudeville jig-dancer, real estate agent, tailor, patent-medicine salesman, "restaurant & bakery" co-proprietor (with his mother, who seems to have been rather an estimable character) and, finally, bartender. That was all by the time he was 30. Oh, and in 1891, when he was 29, he even went so far as to publish a bartending guide, one of the first from the West Coast.*

The *San Francisco Chronicle* documented his passing in August 1930 at age seventy, describing his great influence in the world of cocktails—"probably the best-known bartender in San Francisco in pre-Volstead [Act] days"—and the collection of "old-time bartenders" who came from across the country to show up for duty as pallbearers for their old friend.

> *Old time San Francisco bon vivants, who made the daily pilgrimage along the famous "cocktail route" when Andrew J. Volstead was the comparatively obscure county attorney of Yellow Medicine county, Minnesota, came together again yesterday—but it was for a funeral....Among the downcast faces...were a score who used to greet all comers with a bright smile and a satisfying thirst-slaker out of materials that have become passe or poisonous under the eighteenth amendment.*

While the Boothby cocktail is a true San Francisco original, it's not easily found in cocktail books beyond Boothby's own—a search through my modest collection at home turned up nothing—or even in very many of the city's bars today. Those establishments that set out to honor the local history or classic cocktails are more likely to know what you're talking about if you order one, but that profile is not a guarantee. At Wayfare Tavern—the clubby, pubby restaurant by TV chef Tyler Florence with taxidermied deer heads mounted on its walls and a quote by famous 1914 chronicler of San Francisco dining Clarence Edwords on its menu—a young server was perplexed when I placed the cocktail order (I then explained it as essentially a Manhattan with champagne float); the resulting drink was fine. At the House of Shields, however, with its lack of clock or TV or anything remotely electronic—iPhones don't even seem prevalent with patrons somehow—you can reliably order a Boothby, just that, and get what you came for. It was House of Shields bar manager Eric Passetti who first told me about the drink, and after that conversation, I proceeded on a bit of a Boothby quest, ordering one at a

The Boothby cocktail, Cockscomb, 2017. *Brandon Borrman.*

handful of establishments to see what happened. Comstock Saloon, not surprisingly, also delivered on the request. There, when I inquired if I might have a Boothby, somewhat timidly, thinking the question would be met with a confused look, the expert server replied, "Of course," without flinching. Comstock's was good (its pisco punch is even better), but the House of Shields' rendition is still my favorite—made doubly appropriate for inclusion here, as its creator once worked right across the street at another bar in the Palace Hotel.

One of Boothby's old friends—whether a patron or fellow bartender is unclear—T.E. Collins (of Seattle) was quoted in the *Chronicle*'s obituary on the import and ethereal nature of his friend's signature drink: "The younger generation should have known the famous Boothby Cocktail invented by Bill when he was head bartender at this very hotel. It consisted of a delectable Manhattan, with a champagne float—a drink that never the high gods of Mount Olympus quaffed."

There is not a recipe for the Boothby cocktail in his "how to mix drinks" book, but his recipe for a Manhattan is notable for its equal parts of whiskey to vermouth and other elements not typical in today's mixture.

Boothby's Manhattan Cocktail (No. 26 in his "How to Mix Drinks")

Into a small mixing-glass place one-quarter teaspoonful of sugar, two teaspoonfuls of water, three drops of Angostura, one-half jiggerful of whiskey and one-half jiggerful of vermouth; stir, strain into a small bar glass, twist lemon peel and throw in and serve with ice water on the side.

House of Shields' Boothby Cocktail, courtesy of Eric Passetti

2¾ ounces rye whiskey
¾ ounce Antica Carpano Italian Vermouth
2 dashes Angostura bitters
1 dash orange bitters
1 ounce sparkling wine
Luxardo maraschino cherry to garnish

Combine all ingredients except the sparkling wine and cherry over ice in a mixing glass. Stir until well combined (author's note: because I like them extremely cold, I stir most mixed drinks excessively, more than 100 times around the glass). Strain into a coupe glass. Float the sparkling wine on top; if you want to be fancy, follow the true bartender method of "the float": pour the wine slowly over the back of a bar spoon turned upside down over the drink, gently touching the side of the glass, so the wine sits delicately on the top of the drink. Garnish with a Luxardo cherry, if desired.

Wondrich's recipe that appears on Liquor.com calls for a little less rye and a little more sweet vermouth but is quite similar to what you'd get at the House of Shields, where you can rub elbows with young tech workers and old bar lovers simultaneously, ponder the many eras of the bar that used to have no women's restroom and not think about the passing of time—as there is no clock in the place.

Chapter 9

IT PACKS A (PISCO) PUNCH

(early 1900s, post-1906)

Rudyard Kipling's poetry, a professional bartender, global importer routes and a passionate Peruvian chef who calls San Francisco home—all have in common the perfect garden party drink that packs a super wallop, with serious San Francisco history attached. The pisco punch is a worldly drink, and the city should be proud to assert itself as its originator.

Over the course of researching this book, I met a woman, notably a history buff and member of the local postcard society (there is such a thing), whose e-mail handle was "piscopunch." "So when did you taste your first pisco punch?" I asked. "I didn't have one until after I chose the e-mail!" she laughed, explaining that she loved the fact that it was an iconic city cocktail that many people today don't know about.

I was flabbergasted and excited. This is San Francisco legacy! This is what it's about! This lady didn't even know the taste or effect of the drink but built her whole e-mail around it! I loved it all and couldn't wait to experience the pisco punch for myself—and to hear from the experts who know the drink well.

The pisco punch is so iconic San Franicsco that "perhaps no city's cocktail history is as closely associated with one drink as San Francisco's is with Pisco Punch," says a liquor company website on the subject of the famous "Golden City" drink.

Kipling quotably writes about the cocktail in his 1889 work *From Sea to Sea* with these lighter-than-air words:

compounded of the shavings of cherub's wings,
the glory of a tropical dawn,
the red clouds of sunset
and the fragments of lost epics by dead masters

The "tropical dawn" and "red clouds of sunset" bits throw confusion into the mix when gazing upon most modern renditions of pisco punch: there's typically no red. No orange. Nothing resembling sunsety hues to make sense of that soliloquy. Today, in most bars, the drink looks like fancy lemonade, or perhaps plain-old, regular, sidewalk-stand lemonade, with no hint at its fierce strength. But it contains a lot more than just citrus and sugar in its making.

Pineapple, pisco (a clear, white-grape Peruvian brandy that "first reached San Francisco aboard a ship that Spanish captain Juan Francisco de la Bodega y Quadra had retrofitted to hold the precious casks in the 1700s"),[26] simple syrup or gum arabic and an element of citrus are in the mix, though the actual original recipe is said to have died with its creator—or perhaps, rather, its most famous slinger. Duncan Nicol of the Bank Exchange and Billiard Saloon, on the site of the current Transamerica Pyramid at the tri-street corner of Montgomery, Columbus and Washington, is often credited with the drink, but some say he may have just popularized something created by a previous owner of the bar.

There are many theories about the historical origins of the color, and pisco devotee Duggan McDonnell adheres to original formulations (estimated, as there's no documented recipe for the original concoction that's ever been discovered): his has a deep red hue. Modern barkeep, cocktail educator, entrepreneur and author who wrote a book about San Francisco's cocktails (*Drinking the Devil's Acre*), McDonnell shares his recipe for the historic cocktail. It features his own proprietary pisco (Campo de Encanto Grand & Noble Pisco); homemade pineapple cordial with gum arabic in it; fresh lime juice; a dash of bitters; and, aha, fortified wine Lillet Rouge for the red element. This combination makes the cocktail not at all lemonade-colored but a beautiful deep purple, with a thin layer of froth along the top. His insight into the color is pretty rare.

"I own the only unopened bottle of original Bank Exchange pisco punch known to the world, which states on its front label, 'According to the Original Formula of Duncan Nicol,'" McDonnell states in his book. "The liquid contents inside this relic, though oxidized, have always been a reddish brown. This crimson color had previously perplexed me."

Two local classics (beer and pisco punch) featured side by side on the Regal Amber Lager beer truck, parked next to Garbro Brand building in Sebastopol, California, circa 1920s. *Western Sonoma County Historical Society.*

La Mar pisco punch, 2017. *Brandon Borrman.*

The potency of the original formulation is credited with an ingredient not permissible in legal products today: coca leaves. McDonnell explains his findings:

> *In 1893, the Bordeaux-produced Vin Mariani, a fortified, aromatized red wine infused with coca leaves, captivated the attention of the world. Developed in the 1860s by chemist and health expert Angelo Mariani, Vin Mariani harnessed the magic of the Incas—coca leaves—in his wildly popular aperitif. Soon, many more coca wines followed, being produced in Bordeaux and California alike.*

He recounts how the early 1900s saw a shift in thinking about coca-infused products, as "both the political climate for alcohol was souring and coca was being blamed for various undesirable behaviors." Eventually, coca wines were banned, and the Vin Mariani of the sort Nicol knew was no more. Lillet Rouge became a rightful substitute after it was introduced in 1963, but knowledge of the once-famous cocktail in San Francisco had temporarily gone dormant, as its original generation of fans was no longer alive.

Along with McDonnell, Guillermo Toro-Lira is considered one of the modern experts on pisco and pisco punch, with multiple books on the subject. His first, beautifully named after Kipling's poetry about the drink, *Wings of Cherubs: The Saga of the Rediscovery of Pisco Punch, San Francisco's Mystery Drink*, kicked off a renewal for the cocktail in the city, and Toro-Lira has continued to evangelize for its story. One of the researcher's fans, and a champion for the Peruvian influence on San Francisco cuisine and heritage, is local chef Nico Vera, who has his own blog, does pop-up dinners and cooking classes and is an overall force for all things Peru in the city.

Vera refers to Toro-Lira's book as in the style of magical realism, saying he "learned more about the history of San Francisco than ever before. And now, whenever I am out on the town, I feel more connected to its past." He's "in awe" of the fact that these little patches of the city—in the Mission, North Beach and in the stretch around the Transamerica building that's historically referred to as both the "Monkey Block"[27] and the nearby "Devil's Acre"—"are all connected to the history of pisco, and of course to Peru."

Not only a cheerleader for Peru, Vera is a brilliant storyteller, driven by cultural, familial and historic connections in all that he does. Stories inform his food and his advocacy, and it's impossible not to be affected by his passion for place. We first spoke about pisco punch, a conversation in

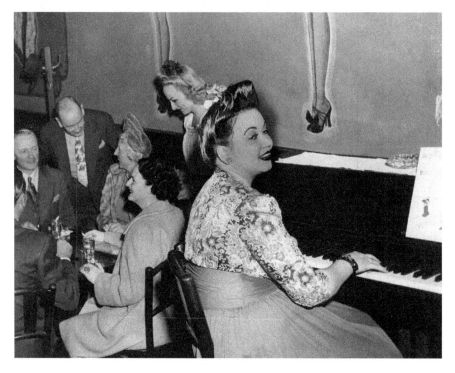

"A congenial bunch enjoys that famous Pisco punch at the House of Pisco, 580 Pacific avenue," says the copy on this image that shows Edith Griffin playing at the House of Pisco, 1942. *San Francisco History Center, San Francisco Public Library.*

which he was extremely deferential to Toro-Lira and McDonnell and all who have dedicated chunks of their lives to researching the drink. But I was most moved by my experience at his Andean feast pop-up dinner, where he presented, among other wonderful dishes, a traditional Peruvian specialty called the Pachamanca, so named after the Andean word for Mother Earth, *Pachamama*, an ancient Incan dish consisting of layers of meat, vegetables and herbs separated by corn husks and cooked in an earthen oven (*pacha* means earth and *manca* means oven). Vera modernized it to suit the cooking opportunities afforded by a 2017 kitchen but maintained the ritual around it for guests. We walked outside to a nearby tree for a brief ceremony honoring Mother Earth before digging into the gorgeously homey, traditional meal. Throughout the evening, he alternated cooking duties with educational opportunities, moving through the room to visit with guests, answer questions about the meal and share his knowledge, humbly and gently, about Peruvian heritage in the city.

Chef Nico Vera, cooking teacher, blogger and champion for Peruvian cuisine, represents the "Pisco Trail" in San Francisco. *Brandon Borrman.*

Afterward, my husband and I drank pisco punches at a fantastic modern spot for Peruvian cuisine, La Mar. Situated on the Embarcadero and stellar with seafood, La Mar offers a pisco punch in the potent lemonade variety. Tart, sweet and packing a wallop, the cocktail is a worthy member of the pantheon. North Beach's Comstock Saloon—an absolute go-to modern spot for dependable and delicious classic cocktails, in old-timey environs to match—offers a similar version, the color a cloudy white tinged with yellow from a hefty piece of lemon peel. The drink is deceptively very, very light, with the delicate quality of an old-fashioned tea party beverage, but about five minutes in, you feel the quiet force behind the cocktail. If you go on a Friday during the day, take advantage of the free lunch special with the purchase of two adult beverages—but beware, two pisco punches might take you under the table for a midday nap.

Pisco Punch Recipe, courtesy of Nico Vera

2 ounces pisco, Italia grape
1 ounce lime juice
1 ounce pineapple gum syrup
½ ounce red aperitif wine
Dash aromatic bitters
One cocktail glass, between 4–6 ounces
An expressed orange peel

Mix the pisco, lime, syrup, wine and bitters in a shaker with ice. Shake vigorously and strain into a chilled cocktail goblet. Garnish with an expressed orange peel.

Chapter 10

FROM BASQUE SHEPHERDS TO NORTH BEACH BARS: PICON PUNCH

(early 1900s)

hat other punch," I found myself saying each time I asked someone about Picon, not pisco, punch. "You know, by the Basques?"

I'd never heard of Picon punch before my friend Eric Passetti—creator, owner and manager of a number of popular bars around the city, with links to the House of Shields, the 166-year-old Old Ship Saloon and most recently Tequila Mockingbird, and a descendant of San Francisco barmen—mentioned it. His passion for history and knowledge of the city's bar scene has been immensely helpful to me now over two book projects. I trust him immensely when it comes to the world of San Francisco spirits.

Eric described Picon punch as a "North Beach classic" until Picon discontinued importing to the United States. "On a recent visit to Gio's house, I noticed a bottle....I got excited!"

Again, he had a hook-up. He told me his friend Gio—short for Giovanni Costabile, a "retired restaurant operator and quasi-SF restaurant historian," best known for his time as proprietor of the eponymous Gio's, a bar and eatery near the Transamerica Pyramid that closed in 2012—knew all about it.

A few weeks later, I met up with Gio and Eric at the Ferry Building, and amidst the bustle of tourists and locals dining, drinking and shopping at one of my favorite spots in town, I got the story—later substantiated with plenty written about the drink.

Picon is a French bitter orange-based liqueur, its history well captured by Veronica Meewes of PUNCH:

Picon punches. *Basque Librarian Iñaki Arrieta Baro at the Jon Bilbao Basque Library, University of Nevada–Reno Library.*

The liqueur was created in 1837 by Gaétan Picon who—after contracting malaria while stationed in Algeria—infused alcohol with dried orange zest, gentian, quinine, sugar syrup and caramel before distilling it. Picon, who had apprenticed at French distilleries before joining the army, already knew a bit about chemistry and attributed his recovery to the botanical blend he'd created. His superiors insisted he continue to produce it for the French troops and, once his tour of duty was over in 1840, he remained in Philippeville (now called Skikda) to open his first distillery.[28]

The name eventually changed as popularity of the liqueur spread:

His Amer Africain ("African bitters") grew to high demand, and Picon soon opened three larger distilleries in Algiers, Constantine and a city now known as Annaba. In 1862, he entered his product into the Universal Exhibition in London, where it won a bronze medal under the "Bitter Appetizers" category, prompting Picon to open a larger distillery in Marseilles and rename his creation Amer Picon.

After Picon's death in 1882, his son and sons-in-law ran his company (by then called the House of Picon), opening branches throughout Europe while still importing oranges from Algeria to create the proprietary blend. Amer Picon began appearing in classic American cocktails around the turn of the century, as evidenced by many of the first bartending books, which contained now-classic recipes for Picon drinks like Brooklyn and the Liberal.

In the United States, the liqueur was embraced by Basque sheepherders in the American West in the late 1880s, primarily in Central California and Nevada. Most origin stories for the punch based on the bitter do not credit San Francisco proper as the birthplace for the cocktail—Bakersfield, California, and Reno, Nevada, both have claims as the originators of the drink—but because of its popularity in an Italian (and also, historically, Basque) part of the City by the Bay, I include it here.

A classic Picon punch involves grenadine; the amount and how it's poured Costabile describes as "controversial," though he says it should be just a few drops. The typical glass used is an Irish coffee glass, filled with a couple ounces of Picon, topped with plain soda, a brandy float and a twist of lemon, always on the rocks.

"Trader Vic" Bergeron offers this recipe in his *Bartender's Guide* from 1947:

> 2 ounces Amer Picon
> 1 teaspoon Grenadine
> 1 dash lemon juice

> Stir with cracked ice; strain into goblet; add cracked ice; twist lemon peel over drink and fill with seltzer. Serve with straws.

Why one would need multiple straws with the drink, I don't know—particularly imagining the traditional vessel, an Irish coffee glass. But Bergeron's street cred makes me trust that there was a reason. He defines a punch in his "Punches and Coolers" chapter introduction: "Punches can be anything from a mild, thin drink to a stinker that will knock you down with a dipperful. There's not much difference between a cooler and a simple, individual punch—just not as much lime or lemon juice in a cooler, which usually calls for just the rinds of lemons or oranges."

And on the use of lemon, he offers that "formulas are changed too often by the use of too much lemon juice....An ounce of lemon juice is ample for any individual drink served in a 10- to 14-ounce glass, but I've seen many a bartender take a bottle of lemon juice and just give a drink a terrific thumping—sometimes as high as 3 ounces. This completely ruins the drink and will upset the most rugged constitution."[29] As a lemon juice lover, making note...

Punches and Coolers 367

PICON PUNCH

2 oz. Amer Picon   1 tsp. grenadine
                    1 dash lemon juice

Stir with cracked ice; strain into goblet; add cracked ice; twist lemon peel over drink and fill with seltzer. Serve with straws.

Image of Trader Vic's recipe for Picon punch from his *Bartender's Guide*. *Brandon Borrman.*

Gio, a gentleman of Italian Mexican descent whose first job was as a seventeen-year-old busboy at the Starlight Room in Union Square circa 1959 ("I faked my way in," he told me), gradually building a life in the restaurant world, culminating with owning his own, could not hide his food-and-drink expertise if he tried. A true representative of a distinguished era of dining, marked by real "table service" that involved a chain of command throughout the front of the house, beginning with maître d' and running through captains, hostesses and waiters—even candy and cigarette girls vending their wares on restaurant floors—Gio knows a lot. Just listening to his tales of San Francisco restaurant yesteryear gave me goosebumps. But I had to focus on the reason for the interview: the Picon punch. He divulged to me a delightful riff on the elixir called a Picadillo, where champagne is substituted for the soda—why not up the booze factor—and cognac in place of brandy. The worthy-sounding alternative follows in a long line of alternate versions of classic cocktails, whereby champagne enters the mix and transforms one drink into another (as in the Boothby, another city legend, a result of a champagne float on a Manhattan) or when one rich liqueur replaces another in a one-to-one fashion (like a brandy Manhattan, where bourbon is left out).

Today, 15 Romolo is the place—and sort of the only place—to go in the city for this classic Picon punch. It is an absolute beaut (the drink, that is), and the building is not too shabby either, with its dark wood, cavernous quality and vintage Edison light bulbs dangling throughout the space, though to step inside at 7:00 p.m. on a Friday in 2017, you're struck more by noise and youthful popularity than you are by the building's roots. Formerly a boardinghouse and restaurant that catered to the Basque community in the city, the Basque Hotel, longtime occupant of a 1912 building on a little alley called Romolo Place, also had stints as a speakeasy and brothel over the years. The bar has kept many historic details intact—even the rooms for sleeping upstairs. The website beckons "roving reporters, enterprising entrepreneurs, and carefree travelers," along with guests of San Francisco residents who may be short on living space, to stay either weekly or monthly in one of the twenty-five private rooms with shared bath. (Such an intriguing Hemingwayesque discovery, this modern boardinghouse over a nice bar just miles from my own home, I've noted its possibility for future immersive writing vacations, should the need arise.)

Another favorite vintage detail not to be missed is the old peephole that remains in the front door, presumably in use not only for boarders but also during the establishment's speakeasy days to ensure all those who would enter were actually welcome.

For decades from the 1940s to the late twentieth century, the Basque Hotel's dining room was hopping, described by *San Francisco Chronicle* reporter Stephen Schwartz in his article just two days after Christmas in 1996, marking the closure of the long establishment:

> *In its heyday, the restaurant's closely packed tables, covered with red and white checkered cloths, were filled. North Beach denizens and aficionados of Basque cuisine, as well as people rooming at the hotel, flocked to the restaurant. They crowded onto the bench seats to dine at tables that were covered with tureens of soup and stew and flagons of robust red wine…. In May 1991,* Chronicle *restaurant reviewer Tom Sietsema described the restaurant as a "vast and affectionately quirky dining room that could pass for a boarding school cafeteria…." The closing of the restaurant in the Basque Hotel, which continues to rent rooms to lodgers, marks the passing of another San Francisco tradition and the continuing decline of the city's Basque community.*[30]

On the occasion of its closure, Schwartz described how the North Beach dining room had long "featured a red, white and green Basque flag and paintings of tranquil fishing scenes and pastoral villages in the Pyrenees" before gradually losing foot traffic up the little alleyway as the city's gustatory customs changed. "And the long-standing custom of serving big, family-style Basque meals—five courses, ranging from pepper pea soup to brandied cake—has ended."

Hotel Vasco, Basque Hotel in San Francisco, 1870. *Jon Bilbao Basque Library, University of Nevada–Reno Library.*

San Francisco had become a central hub for Basque immigrants to the United States for a variety of reasons. Schwartz describes how the population swelled in the city after the Spanish Civil War ended in 1939, with Basques fleeing the region. Schwartz discusses how the Basque community became so sizable in the city over the years that it eventually created a "buffer zone of Basque hotels and restaurants" between Chinatown and the Italian enclave of North Beach. "The North Beach 'Basquetown' was a business community providing lodgings and family-style meals to sheepherders and others migrating on a circuit from San Francisco, the 'capital' of the Amerikanuak, or American Basques, to Idaho, Nevada and southern California," he reports.

So the Basque Hotel was just one of many similar establishments in midcentury San Francisco until migration slowed and the Basque population dwindled, diminishing demand for the homey multipurpose businesses.

In 1998, two years after the Basque Hotel's closure as a restaurant, the building at 15 Romolo was bought by the current owners and revitalized, and its original business, sans the family-style dinners and prostitutes, was revived.

Members of the San Francisco Basque community at the Panama-Pacific International Exposition, 1915. *Jon Bilbao Basque Library, University of Nevada–Reno Library.*

"Twenty years ago, the cocktail scene was barely being reborn in places like New York and San Francisco," assistant manager Andrew Meltzer told me. "Romolo looked a little different, was less busy, less occupied at the time. It was essentially a hole in the wall up an old alleyway, with Jäger shots and Red Bull and all the other late '90s things."

But the new owners were also "doing things with fresh juices and syrups and great produce," Meltzer shared, "paying more attention to detail than some of their peers."

After a "facelift" about ten years ago that involved "tearing up the Cookie Monster–blue banquette seating" and renovating and reopening the kitchen, 15 Romolo and the Basque Hotel is now a buzzing tavern once again—though brandied cake, sadly, does not appear on the menu. It serves "mostly creative bar food," as Meltzer puts it, intentionally targeting a late-night dining experience for fellow industry peeps—chefs, servers and "otherwise hungry neighborhood folks"—whose schedules trend a little later than the rest of the city. It has a special sherry program, featuring sherry-based cocktails, pairings for every menu item and an annual Christmas sherry menu.

"It is an excellent modifier, so it usually plays along with another base spirit, like gin, brandy, tequila, whiskey or vodka or rum," Meltzer says of sherry. "But it also works well on its own as the basis for low-proof cocktails," something the establishment is passionate about for the way the replacement of soda water for another base spirit can both lower the proof, making a drink better for pairing, and add hydration, enabling greater productivity for the drinker.

Its signature drink, on the other hand, is not low-proof and plays a somewhat demure role on the menu, tucked away in the upper right corner of the oversized cardstock under "Happy Hour" specials, teensy, almost apologetic. But it should be ordered, repeatedly, let out of its little corner to sing sweetly and bitterly, at once, a deep, rich, reddish-brandy brown in its elegant Irish coffee glass, on your perfect wood-grain table. The 15 Romolo Picon punch, which Meltzer describes as "like a black Manhattan," is a gorgeous, captivating little cocktail, tasting of bitter orange (the origin of the Picon liqueur) and brandy, its flavors rounded with house-made grenadine and lightened with a splash of seltzer.

Meltzer and his 15 Romolo colleagues—including general manager Ian Adams and marketing manager Valter Fabiano—shared their special recipe for the cocktail, which has also made an appearance online via fabulous drink magazine PUNCH.[31] Meltzer emphasizes the importance of using just a drop of grenadine—"you don't want to sweeten it too much because it's already a sweet liqueur"—and the real stuff, made of real pomegranate juice, sugar, pomegranate molasses "for body" and a perfumey note of orange flower water, rather than the bright-red Rose's version most people know. "This element will make or break the cocktail," Meltzer says.

This one's a revelation for me in the research for this book. I am hooked upon first sip, and the Picon punch is now part of my personal cocktail lexicon. Though I can't imagine it tasting better than what the guys at 15 Romolo have cooked up behind their bar, you can order the punch with the original Amer Picon for an extra five dollars. (They keep a secret stash, as does nearby Comstock Saloon, but the latter is in plain view on the barroom wall, notably in a locked glass case.)

These days, 15 Romolo sells the most Picon punches at happy hour, a time when an opportunity for real reflection arises. "It often sparks a conversation between bartender and guest about the history of the space, the hotel, the many different chefs we've had and some of the fun stories in our history books," Meltzer says.

And other than the little annual neighborhood Basque fair and a fleeting, subpar Picon punch on a few other bar menus, 15 Romolo is one of few remaining representatives of the city's Basque legacy. "I think it's really cool that we've been able to hold on to a little bit of the history that's otherwise faded, seeing as how most people come to the area for the touristy parts of Chinatown and Little Italy," Meltzer says.

Thank you to Eric, Gio, Andrew, Ian and Valter for bringing me into the world of Picon and this lesser-known part of San Francisco's history. And especially to Andrew, for this pro tip: one of the best times to sit and enjoy a Picon punch at the bar is on a Sunday at 3:00 p.m., listening to Count Basie and watching the neighborhood go by.

15 Romolo Picon Punch
Serves 1

1 ½ ounce Basque Picon (see 15 Romolo's Picon, below)
¼ ounce grenadine (made in-house at 15 Romolo)
Ice
1 ounce soda water, chilled
½ ounce brandy, Spanish
Lemon twist to garnish

In a small cocktail or Irish coffee glass, combine Picon, grenadine and ice and stir briefly. Top with soda water and float brandy on top. Garnish with a lemon twist.

15 Romolo's Basque Picon

In an airtight bottle, combine 4 parts Ramazzotti, 2 parts Pierre Ferrand dry curaçao and 1 part Avèze gentian liqueur. Refrigerate until ready to use.

Chapter 11

THE OPERATIC ROOTS OF A HUMBLE HOME COOK'S DISH: CHICKEN TETRAZZINI

(early 1900s)

Named for an opera singer, this dish best known as a use for Thanksgiving leftovers is a midcentury home cook's hit that figured prominently in my childhood. A contributor to Food 52[32] describes it as "as retro as it gets" and shares how his mother used to "prepare an elaborate entrée and then serve it with a convenience side like Birds Eye Beans and Spaetzle." Betty Crocker has a version that I most relate to; Google search results entice with this description: "Enjoy this creamy chicken and mushroom spaghetti casserole—a hearty pasta dinner recipe for your family." And it's a description that jibes with my memories.

The modern versions all are riffs on the classic, but with fill-in-the-blank proteins (chicken, the super-common post-Thanksgiving turkey, even salmon), and all share the common thread of cream, mushrooms and pasta. And an opera singer.

What the historical accounts of the dish (read on) don't capture is why chicken, why mushrooms, why creaminess, why pasta. Is it because opera singer Luisa Tetrazzini was Italian, so Palace Hotel chef Ernest Arbogast imagined what he thought would be the most unctuous, most indulgent, most reverent version of an Italian pasta in her honor? Or is there something more? Did Tetrazzini herself love mushrooms? Or creamy pasta? These are the questions I am still determined to get answers to (recall what I said in the introduction about the lingering mysteries of history).

I learned a lot, however, from Erica Peters, founder of Culinary Historians of Northern California and author of the incredible work documenting the city's foodways, *San Francisco: A Food Biography*.

Luisa Tetrazzini (*left*) in front of the San Francisco Chronicle Building on Christmas Eve 1910, *Album of San Francisco*, vol. 1, p. 173. *California History Room, California State Library, Sacramento, California.*

Origin claims to the dish are somewhat split between San Francisco and New York, as it seems with many famous dishes or drinks in this vicinity (the martini at the top of the hotly disputed list); Peters notes in her seminal work and reiterated to me that the earliest printed documentation of the dish she could find uses turkey and appears in an issue of *Good Housekeeping* magazine in October 1908 and makes reference to a New York restaurant, "on Forty-second Street." (She confessed: "That's not determinative; dishes don't always make it into a publication when they're invented. But I tried hard to find proof of a San Francisco origin for my book (naturally!) and I came up empty.") The entry explains that the dish is named after the famous singer and involves "cooked turkey in a cream sauce," with spaghetti, "a little grated cheese" and "very thin slices of mushrooms cut crossways." The description reveals a casserole-style dish, complete with browned bread crumbs on top. Peters posits the restaurant to likely be the Knickerbocker Hotel at Forty-Second and Broadway in Manhattan, frequent home to famous opera singers.

The San Francisco story goes that after a 1910 impromptu outdoor concert in front of the Chron (San Francisco Chronicle to nonlocals) building, famed

Italian opera singer Luisa Tetrazzini was honored by the local chef of the Palace Hotel, Ernest Arbogast, with the creation of this comfort food dish. Perhaps he was inspired by her feistiness—she defied managers and contract owners by "singing in the streets" for the people, an estimated 250,000 to be exact—or maybe he loved her girth and imagined she was one who loved her food and drink. Peters also shares a wonderful quote by Tetrazzini herself, from the March 20, 1921 issue of the *San Francisco Call*, that makes her sound like the previous incarnation of Julia Child and Paula Deen combined:

> *I thrive on butter and eggs. As for spaghetti, I often eat it twice daily. Sometimes I drink a pint of rich cream at one meal. I revel in olive oil, not only because I like the taste, but because it is good for the muscles of the throat....Think of trying to go through "Lucia" or "Rigoletto" on a luncheon of lettuce and a glass of lemonade—it could never be done.*

Locating some form of tetrazzini on a Bay Area menu in the new millennium proves challenging but not impossible. Going outside the seven-by-seven-mile perimeter of the city enabled greater success in discovering

Platform in front of the Chronicle Building erected for Luisa Tetrazzini's Christmas Eve performance, 1910. *Album of San Francisco*, vol. 1, p. 375. *California History Room, California State Library, Sacramento, California.*

the dish today—a substantial forty-five miles outside, all the way to Livermore. A traditionally pastoral town on the outskirts of the Bay Area, Livermore has seen a boom in its wine industry over the last twenty years, with vineyards and tasting rooms popping up in surrounding areas, and a population explosion to go with it. A newcomer to the Livermore restaurant scene, a scene not comparable in volume or stature to San Francisco, but with proper dining emerging nevertheless, Americano Cucino Trattoria and Grill offers a version called "La Famiglia Tetrazzini," which resembles the original preparation.

Back in the city, acclaimed local chef turned Food Network culinary superstar Chris Cosentino, who gained fame with his commitment to meats and offal (through whole-beast restaurant Incanto and charcuterie purveyor Boccalone, RIP), served tetrazzini on his 2014 inaugural menu at Cockscomb, a restaurant established in 2014 that shows consistent reverence to the city's classic dishes. His version used quail, less common in suburban American home kitchens, but stuck to the original flavors of the dish.

"I didn't want to do per se a classic pasta dish," Cosentino said. "So I thought a lot about what made tetrazzini unique and how can I incorporate the same flavors into the dish." He used quail for the poultry element, traditional mushrooms and crème fraiche for the creamy part but substituted fideo (angel hair–like noodles) for the spaghetti. "Two birds on the plate, a little bit of thyme, very clean," he recounts of the presentation. At the time of our interview, Cosentino said he would be bringing back the tetrazzini in the new year; cannot wait to try it.

Also on that inaugural menu were Celery Victor, a green goddess salad with little gem lettuces and, as today, lots of iconic San Francisco cocktails. There's also a collection of house drinks named for movies set in the city, some famous (like Bullitt) and some more obscure (um, Kuffs). The chef's affinity for the city's classics is clear and goes beyond his own restaurant menus; he even did a version of Celery Victor for a *Saveur* magazine dinner that featured white truffles and celery root, buried in embers, chilled and then sliced thin on a meat slicer to create ribbons of roasted root. The final preparation added raw, shaved celery and bias-cut celery, picked celery leaves, parsley and champagne vinegar and was garnished with crispy chicken skin.

"We screamed gold, and everybody came. Chinese, Portuguese, French, Spanish, Italian, English—and they all brought with them their food," he reflects on the city's historic culinary character, a powerful draw (along with a childhood love of *Starsky & Hutch*) for this Rhode Island native to his chosen hometown. This legacy of immigrants and a diverse culinary landscape is part of what he honors in his restaurant today. "For me, it's really about celebrating San Francisco through San Francisco food—not Cal-French or Cal-Med. San Francisco is distinct and unique to its own."

The importance of history comes through in his approach to food.

"You can't run a marathon if you run around the block twice," he says. "You have to have the legs to stand on. It's the same thing with cooking. If you don't know your history and you can't understand where the food comes from and why it's the way it is, then everything becomes lost in translation to the guest."

He's enamored by San Francisco and concerned the city might be losing hold of what has made it special for so long. "So many people moved here because of its uniqueness, but I'm afraid for us to lose that," he said. "There's so much cool stuff, so many great things. I think it's really important to understand time and place, and just really respect where you're from. Granted, I'm from Rhode Island, but this is home. This is beautiful. And I love it here."

And about home: I'd say that's the best place to enjoy a good chicken or turkey tetrazzini. It's the first and likely only place most people have had the dish, and it remains the perfect environment for tucking into this classic casserole. Though when I have a hankering for a version prepared by a celebrity chef, seated at a butcher block table, surrounded by pumping music, mounted animal heads and historic San Francisco culinary tributes, I'll head to Cockscomb.

Oakland Thanksgiving Leftovers 2017 Turkey Tetrazzini

Long a fan of tetrazzini and all its variations, I adapted a recipe from Genius Kitchen[33] this year after turkey day, and it was a huge hit with my children. The author notes it was an adaptation from a Cooking Light recipe (I've removed all "light" and "low-fat" notations because I don't keep low-fat cheese in the house, but feel free to use whatever you have on hand). As with so many great recipes, here's another layer of adjustment.

Ready in a little more than an hour.

Serves 6

1 tablespoon butter
½ cup finely chopped onion
⅓ cup finely chopped celery

½ teaspoon ground pepper
½ teaspoon salt
¾ cup roughly chopped baby carrots
8 ounces sliced mushrooms (optional; I traditionally include mushrooms but didn't
have them in the house this go-round, and it was surprisingly fine)
½ cup flour
½ cup white wine (or sherry)
4 cups broth (chicken or turkey would work here)
I cup parmesan cheese (divided)
½ cup shredded Monterey jack, cheddar or colby cheese (whatever
you have handy)
3 to 4 ounces cream cheese
¾ cup frozen peas
2 cups turkey meat, cooked and chopped (or chicken)
8 ounces spaghetti or linguine (cooked)
¾ cup panko breadcrumbs

Preheat oven to 350. Melt butter in sauté pan. Add onion, celery, pepper, salt, carrots and mushrooms (optional). Sauté until vegetables are tender.

Add flour and stir until vegetables are coated (you're making a little roux here). Add wine and stir quickly until flour is absorbed. Gradually add broth, stirring constantly. Bring to a boil, reduce heat and simmer 5 minutes, stirring frequently. Remove from heat.

Add ½ cup Parmesan cheese, ¼ cup shredded jack or cheddar and the cream cheese, stirring until cheese melts. Add the peas, turkey and pasta. Stir until blended. Coat a casserole with nonstick spray and transfer mixture to the casserole.

Combine panko with remaining Parmesan cheese and jack or cheddar cheese. Sprinkle mixture evenly over the top of the casserole. Bake at 350 for 30 to 40 minutes until lightly browned. Let rest for 15 minutes before serving.

Chapter 12

ASCETIC DELIGHT: CELERY VICTOR

(1910)

I t's weird, wormlike, salty and delicious. It does not try to impress. And it's something I'm fairly certain my grandmother would have secretly loved, not unlike her treasured liver and onions, against my grandpa's wishes. I love everything about it.

The dish in question is the Celery Victor, truly an ascetic culinary delight. What I mean is that it feels austere, certainly in look, like a self-denial of some sort of gustatory pleasure (but deliciousness is there, I promise). The dish is a unique representative of the era of dining in San Francisco when European chefs were at the helms of hotel kitchens and fresh produce was harder to come by. Or less revered. Whatever it was, something spurred Alsatian chef Victor Hirtzler of the Hotel St. Francis circa 1910 to create this gem of a "salad"—and I use the term loosely, as it does not resemble a crunchy combination of mostly raw ingredients most people think of as salad today. Hirtzler divulged the recipe to food writer Clarence Edwords, eventually included it in his 1919 *Hotel St. Francis Cook Book* and it gradually became a San Francisco thing.

Los Angeles Times writer Barbara Hansen captured the spirit of the dish on the occasion of the reprinting of Hirtzler's famous cookbook in 1988: "There was a time when California cuisine did not mean goat cheese, grilled anything, baby produce and the rest of today's trendy ideas. In the past, some remarkable cooking took place in this state, dishes virtually forgotten in the contemporary rush toward smart new foods."[34]

Tasting the dish today amid all the "trendy ideas"—and it's near impossible to find on San Francisco restaurant menus—makes its initial appeal and inspiration unobvious. Culinary historian Erica Peters theorizes what may have prompted the flamboyant chef—he was known for his red fez—to develop it:

> *San Francisco's celery customs may have been a sore spot for this classically trained chef. In the early twentieth century, San Franciscans expected celery on the table among the hors d'oeuvres, and celery was always on the table at Thanksgiving. Aside from using it for stuffing or cream of celery soup, diners expected to eat celery raw. French people, on the other hand, had much less enthusiasm for raw produce. By cooking celery in a rich, meaty stock, Hirtzler tamed this crunchy vegetable and made it acceptable to a more sophisticated palate, which meant, in his view, a French-trained palate. Signaling the success of Hirtzler's approach, Celery Victor soon became fashionable at Thanksgiving and Christmas banquets across San Francisco.*[35]

Hirtzler's original recipe appears on a single page in the hotel's cookbook of 1919, which the hotel (now the Westin St. Francis) keeps in a locked glass display case in the lobby today, as well as a second tattered copy purchased by someone, according to the notation, secondhand for $3.50. That copy is kept by chef de cuisine Thomas Rimpel in his office, deep in the backstage area of the kitchen behind the glossy front of the house of the hotel.

Victor Hirtzler's Original Method for Celery Victor

Wash six stalks of large celery. Make a stock with one soup hen or chicken bones and five pounds of veal bones in the usual manner with carrots, onions, bay leaves, parsley, salt, and whole pepper. Place celery in vessel and strain broth over same, and boil until soft. Allow to cool in the broth. When cold, press the broth out of the celery gently with the hands, and place on plate. Season with salt, fresh-ground black pepper, chervil, and one-quarter white wine tarragon vinegar to three-quarters of olive oil.[36]

Fascinatingly, Celery Victor appears in the 1915 *Pan-Pacific Cook Book* as well, predating the print of Hirtzler's official version in the *Hotel St. Francis Cook Book*. It varies significantly from the original, with the addition of French dressing made tangier with a touch of vinegar and catsup, and notably, the world's fair version features anchovies:

> Trim the outer stalks and leaves from two small heads of celery, leaving them about five inches long, attached to the root. Boil in broth until tender; then drain on a cloth and cut in quarters, through the root, lengthwise, and chill. Fifteen minutes before serving pour over them half a cup of French dressing mixed with a teaspoon each of tarragon vinegar, sweetened tomato catsup and a teaspoon of paprika. Arrange each on a plate and garnish with several anchovy fillets laid in a row on each.[37]

Today at the Westin St. Francis, history is still revered, though the Celery Victor is no longer on the everyday menu. But oddball devotees like me may ask for it, and with enough notice (as the poaching and overall process takes some time), their wishes may be granted. So says Chef Rimpel.

After more than thirty-seven years with the hotel, Rimpel has seen countless dishes come and go and has done his own takes on the classics. His version of the Celery Victor puts shellfish front and center for some heft and complicates the presentation a bit with things like miniature diced cubes of aspic, with which the celery has also been poached. The hotel has featured the dish on various occasions over the last couple of decades, including on a historic menu honoring its 110th anniversary in 2014, with this language:

Victor Hirtzler's St. Francis Celery Victor

> With a red fez set rakishly atop his head and a persona larger than life, chef Victor Hirtzler—native of Strasbourg, France, former taster for Czar Nicholas II and once chef to King Carlos I of Portugal—reigned over the Hotel St. Francis in San Francisco from 1904 to 1926. Among the astonishingly varied, European-inspired creations Hirtzler named after himself, Celery Victor (circa 1910) may be the most enduring. The simple and delicious poached vegetable dish hails from the days before raw greens defined a salad. We've added shrimp for substance and capers for spark.

Even if you're not into an obscure celery dish, the St. Francis is worth visiting for its thoughtful food, elegant architecture and historic place in the city's story. Edwords captures the fierce spirit of the hotel after the 1906 earthquake, when "all that part of the city was a mass of seething flames":

Before business in the down-town district was reorganized, and while the work of removing the tangled masses of debris was still in progress the Merchants Association of San Francisco called its members together in its annual banquet, and this banquet was held in the basement of the Hotel St. Francis, the crumbling walls, and charred and blackened timbers hidden under a mass of bunting and foliage and flowers. Here was emphasized the spirit of Bohemian San Francisco, and it was one of the most merry and enjoyable of feasts ever held in the city.[38]

One hundred years later, Rimpel and his team are the passionate bunch who put out beautiful dishes for parties large and small each day. His reverence for the hotel's history is clear in his menus and the way he treasures the original copy of Hirtzler's cookbook. The culinary team also lends to the marvelous, magical environment at Christmastime: pastry staff begin constructing an incredible gingerbread house each year months before the season.

Today, Sam's Grill on Belden Place is the only restaurant I know of to offer Celery Victor on its regular daily menu. Returning to my initial

Postcard showing café at the St. Francis Hotel, date unknown. *Lauren Thor.*

description in the opening of this chapter, the dish is not much of a looker. When I placed it in front of my husband to take a photograph, I asked, "Aren't you inspired?"

"Oh boy. Yes," he said sarcastically.

"This is the only place in the city that still has it on the menu!" I enthused. To which he responded, "I can't imagine why."

So, it's a special dish. Hard to love by the masses. But once you taste it, if you like intensely salty anchovies, balanced with a fresh pop of a sweet garden tomato and celery that tastes like it's soaked up a really good, homey soup over hours and hours, then this is your dish.

Chapter 13

COMFORT FOOD MASQUERADING AS SALAD: CRAB LOUIS

(1908)

You'd be hard-pressed to walk into a classic restaurant in San Francisco these days and not find a version of a Louis—or Louie; you'll see both spellings—salad on the menu. Often with a basket of sourdough bread nearby, the salad that eats like a meal features one of the city's other great treasures: Dungeness crab. If it's a good one. (It can be made expertly with shrimp or prawns as well, but really, why hold back when you can reach for the stars?) Best considered a vehicle for primo fresh crab in season, the traditional salad has a simple composition: iceberg lettuce, a lightly spiced Thousand Island–style dressing (but different) and succulent, fresh crab. Its history, though, like everything else in this book, is not quite as straightforward.

Several famous and bygone restaurants lay claim to the dish: Solari's Grill on Geary Street (noted as a favorite by *San Francisco Chronicle* restaurant critic Clarence Edwords); the Old Poodle Dog, from multiple streets and so many iterations that when I came across archival material for the restaurant the librarians asked if I was writing a whole book on the place (maybe someday); and the St. Francis Hotel. It was the Bergez-Frank's Old Poodle Dog's 1908 special menu item for Crab Leg a la Louis that caught the attention of historians—which commands mine in turn.

"The restaurant's chef, Louis Coutard, apparently made a specialty of serving crab with chili sauce. Coutard had long been the chef at Frank's Rotisserie [a Poodle Dog predecessor]," documented Erica Peters. Two years before the dish appeared on the Poodle Dog menu, Frank's Rotisserie joined forces with Bergez's Restaurant and the Old Poodle Dog to form a super restaurant: Frank-Bergez's Old Poodle Dog Co. When Coutard, who

Wednesday, October 30th

House of Shields
Bar & Grill
Since 1908

Bar Food
Wed - Fri 4-8pm

SALADS

Mixed Greens	4.50
w/Bleu Cheese	5.50
Caesar	7.50
Tomato Avocado w/Vinaigrette	5.95
Grilled Chicken Breast	9.95
w/ Bacon & Avocado	

APPETIZERS

Fried Calamari	4.95
Fried Prawns	5.95
Proscuitto & Melon	5.95
Prawn Cocktail	5.95
Pate Maison	5.95
Onion Rings 3.25 • GarlicBread 2.75	
Smoked Salmon w/ Rye Toast	6.95

SOUPS	Cup	Bowl
Split Pea	2.50	3.50
French Onion		4.50

TODAY' SPECIALS

Veal Roast w/ Sauteed Potatoes & Madiera Sauce	10.95
Coq Au Vin - Marinated Chicken in Red Wine Sauce w/ Mashed Potatoes	9.95
German Pork Roast w/ Red Cabbage, Potato Pancakes & Apple Sauce	9.95
Old Fashioned Meat Loaf w/ Mushroom Sauce	8.95
Grilled Swordfish w/ Lemon Butter & Mashed Potatoes	10.95
Fettuccini Marinara w/ Scallops & Prawns	10.95
Prawn Louie Salad w/ Avocado, Tomato & Hard Boiled Egg	9.95
Sauteed Breast of Chicken with Caper Sauce	9.95
Autumn Salad - Bosc Pear, Pecans, Arugala & Bleu Cheese	9.95
Salade Nicoise - Albacore, Green Beans, Olives, Red Potato & Egg	9.95
Veal Piccata w/ Rice	9.95
Sauteed Scallops w/ Rice	10.95
Deep Fried Scallops w/ French Fries & Cole Slaw	10.95
Grilled Salmon w/ Fine Herbs	10.95
Pork Tenderloin w/ Porto Wine Sauce & Mashed Potatoes	9.95
Petit Filet Mignon w/ Sauteed Mushrooms	10.95

Even famous bars have had a Louie on their menus, as proven by this vintage menu from the House of Shields—in the days when it served food. *Eric Passetti.*

had been a partner in the new group, died in 1908, his colleagues "honored his invention by listing the dish under his name," says Peters, explaining how two years later, St. Francis Hotel chef Victor Hirtzler published a recipe for Crab a La Louise, which featured sweet Spanish pimentos instead of the chili sauce. Peters continues:

> *The taste for Crab Louis soon spread all over the city. San Franciscans already associated Dungeness crab with celebrations—crab season usually opened either in early November or early December, so locals traditionally enjoyed crab for the holidays. White-aproned vendors on Fisherman's Wharf boiled fresh crab in large kettles and sold it to passersby: a familiar sight to locals, but picturesque enough for a tourist's postcard.*[39]

Local crab fervor at the holidays is still true today. My husband and I have started our own Christmas crab tradition involving multiple presentations

Crab cookers at San Francisco's Fisherman's Wharf, postcard, circa 1938. *California History Room, California State Library, Sacramento, California.*

of the delicious delicacy—first, steamed, picked and presented in a neat little dish alongside a large bowl of chopped crisp romaine, next to a smaller bowl of creamy pink pickle-studded dressing for a Louis-style salad; with a second more indulgent option, like the incredible savory baked tart my husband made last year. When the air chills and the leaves start to fall in the Bay Area, it just feels like Dungeness crab should be on the celebratory dinner table.

Crab Louis itself has taken hold in the imaginations and recipe collections of famous chefs, food personalities and media outlets across the country, firmly established now as one of those modernish American dishes that's been around but no one really knows much about where it came from.

Today, you can find versions of the Louis recipe on websites for Martha Stewart, the Food Network, *Saveur* and the *New York Times*, all featuring some amalgamation of seafood, a mayonnaise-based dressing (often with ketchup or chili sauce) and crisp lettuce. Tamar Adler presented an unusual take on the formula in 2016, omitting the ketchup/chili sauce element altogether. Though I can't be down with that—my persistent child-of-the-'70s-and-'80s-inside screaming, "More ketchup, please!"—I love what she says about the salad itself:

Vintage menu from "one of the best restaurants in San Francisco" in its day, Ernie's restaurant. *Author's collection.*

Somehow Crab Louis has gotten stuck in a corner reserved for kitsch, even as we Americans scuttle along, looking for filling, artful salads at midday and dinnertime and the hours in between. I would release Louis to the tides of time, except that it's such a good meal for a summer night, and such a simple way to mix the luxe with the plain. And I can't think of a better dish to sit down to with a small group of friends with whom you like to talk of things other than how you made what you're eating.[40]

She deems her ketchup-less version "a rather perfect meal for a summer night," which, frankly, still holds true with the ketchup.

In San Francisco today, Crab Louis is everywhere: John's Grill, Sam's Grill, all the grills; all the big old elegant hotels (St. Francis, the Palace); and the Cliff House, of course, where you'll get a delicious Louis with a side of best-view-ever. Many people cite Swan Oyster Depot, powerhouse seafood purveyor with a teensy raw bar—suited to accommodate just about a dozen people at a time—as having the best version, which adds chopped black olives. Notably, the Sancimino family, who runs the place, claim the Louis recipe to be the original, bequeathed by a former customer eons ago who happened to be a hotel chef rumored to have invented it.[41]

Crab Louie at John's Grill, 2017. *Brandon Borrman.*

One of my most exciting discoveries in this book was for a new favorite Louis from a gorgeous hot spot that was bestowed an unusual honor by *Bon Appétit* magazine, which named it the "Best Designed Restaurant of the Year." The hotspot is Leo's Oyster Bar, a super pricey but so worth it gem that leaves you feeling sexier, your taste buds more stimulated, your belly more full of fresh seafood than I can remember any other restaurant doing for me in recent memory. Save your pennies and plan a night out in the city. Andrew Knowlton, as always, says it well: "There are no bad seats or unflattering angles at this gorgeous oyster bar. Instead, there's just you, your date, two glasses of Champagne, and a universe of rose-colored onyx bartops, vintage glassware, shell-shaped wall sconces, and tropical palm wallpaper. It's a *Mad Men* set you get to drink in."[42]

He's so right: upon setting foot in the place, I felt bathed in a soft, glowing light. And immediately thought of Don Draper. It was like stepping into a 1950s dream, full of martinis and oysters and curated beauty. Note that the way-back room is a tiki-themed surprise, different than the rest of the lush decor but not lesser—and perfect for sipping the house mai tai along with your platter of bivalves. I also love, love, love that they feature a menu item called the "Liquid Lunch," a spotlight for the bracingly cold martini as it should be, served with a pile of perfectly pickled vegetables, as an oyster house should have. Be sure to also get the Leo's deviled egg starter with a wing-fried oyster on top. Oh my gracious, you will wish you ordered ten.

Left: Front entry to the gorgeous Leo's Oyster House, 2017. *Brandon Borrman.*

Right: Crab Louie at Leo's Oyster House, 2017. *Brandon Borrman.*

And about that Crab Louis: it's a zinger.

Spicy! Super spicy.

"Well, that's surprising," said my friend Cori after she took a bite. We all loved it. The dressing is just shy of unbearably spicy, in my book—making it precisely what you want in a Louis. This is its differentiator from Thousand Island, and this is what makes it something you feel almost desperate to eat. Creamy, tangy, eggy and slightly sweet, the spice harkens the dish's chili sauce roots and goes so well with fresh seafood (Leo's offers either king crab, rock shrimp or both in the dish), you wonder why there's any other way— besides just drawn butter—to enjoy crustaceans. Executive chef Jennifer Puccio—who leads the culinary program for the Big Night Restaurant Group, which also counts Marlowe, Petit Marlowe and Park Tavern among its slate of properties—graciously shared her recipe. The secret to the spice: that miraculous California ingredient, Sriracha hot sauce. And pickled jalapeños, because a single source of heat just isn't sufficient.

Make this at home in the summer with shrimp or in winter crab season in San Francisco and brace yourself for that moment when you realize that salad—when loaded with seafood and a killer spiced dressing—can be the perfect food.

Leo's Louie Salad

Courtesy of Big Night Restaurant Group and executive chef Jennifer Puccio

Louie Dressing (makes approximately 16–20 portions)
3½ cups mayonnaise
1 cup ketchup
¼ cup grainy mustard
¼ cup Sriracha
½ cup chives
½ cup parsley
¼ cup capers
¼ cup gherkins
½ cup sauerkraut
¼ cup pickled jalapeño
4 hard-boiled eggs

Combine the first 5 ingredients in a bowl. Put the rest of the ingredients except the hard-boiled eggs into the bowl of the food processor and pulse, frequently scraping the sides of the bowl until finely diced, not pureed. Add the eggs to the food processor and pulse until small dice. Add to the contents of the bowl and adjust for salt and black pepper.

Assemble the salad (serves 2 people).

¼ cup shaved fennel
½ cup shredded romaine
Juice from ½ a lemon
Salt to taste
¼ cup mache
¼ cup shaved radish
2 tablespoons tobiko
1 hard-boiled egg, sieved
¼ to ½ cup of prepared Louie dressing (above)
For the seafood: chef's choice; guidance is to use approximately ½ cup per salad
(suggest either rock shrimp, crab or bay shrimp, or a combo)

Combine the fennel and romaine. Dress with the lemon juice and salt and arrange on the plate. Dress the mache and shaved radish with lemon juice and salt and arrange over the top of the lettuce. Sprinkle with tobiko and the sieved egg. Serve with Louie dressing and seafood on the side.

Chapter 14

JOE'S SPECIAL: A MEATY BEAUTY

(1920s)

Marie Duggan is a proud woman. But incredibly humble. Attuned to the ebbs and flows of the restaurant business—and the challenges a generational one can face when it lasts for eighty years—this second-generation Original Joe's matriarch is grateful the restaurant is still going strong. It has survived neighborhood degradation, a devastating fire, a relocation and rebirth and now three ownership changes—all in the same family. All throughout, Joe's has maintained its devotion to the people of San Francisco, from the working class to the elite. To good, rib-sticking Italian food. To a welcoming environment for all. And to its employees, many of whom have been with the restaurant for decades.

On the origin of the Joe's Special, a fantastically delicious and delightfully simple home cook–style dish made of ground beef, spinach and eggs, Marie can't say for sure how it was born. "We know it's a Joe's thing. We know that much."

The most credible of the various theories around its invention relate to a late-night meal for a musician (or a few) dining at New Joe's who wanted a heartier version of a spinach omelet. The chef obliged by adding leftover hamburger from the dinner service, and voila, a classic was born. Closely aligned with that but a simpler explanation is that the dish was invented by a chef at Original Joe's late one night, as many dishes are born. Though the Joe's Special is always a combination of spinach, beef and eggs, its variations are as diverse as the number of restaurants that serve it—and they span far reaches of the Greater Bay Area (you can even get a Joe's Special in the far

Dining room at Original Joe's, home of the Joe's Special, 2017. *Brandon Borrman.*

East Bay town of San Ramon, and I wouldn't be surprised to see it on a menu even in Sacramento). Some takes are extremely eggy (not my preference) or have such a small amount of spinach it appears to be an herbal seasoning rather than a vegetable and primary ingredient. My favorite remains the original. More on that later…

First, about the restaurant itself. Marie's father, Ante "Tony" Rodin, was a Croatian immigrant whose mother died in childbirth just before World War I began. Rodin worked in the galley as part of the merchant marines as a young teenager, eventually traveling to America in his twenties. Once in San Francisco, he lived in a building at the corner of Union and Stockton Streets, just opposite Washington Square Park. He worked at Lucca Restaurant, a popular place in the city through much of the twentieth century, eventually moving on to what began the Joe's concept: Joe's Lunch, a little lunch counter operated by a friend. Then New Joe's was born, "a real restaurant" outgrowth of the lunch counter. A falling out between the owners of New Joe's led a couple of them to strike out on their own with a restaurant after the original, so they called it Original Joe's. It's confusing to have the "new" predate the "original," but that's the way it went. There were so many people involved in the collection of Joe's, including several named Frank, that it's hard to keep straight who owned what. But what is clear is that the lunch counter was first, and it was Tony Rodin and four other partners who opened the Original. And "it is widely accepted as the real, bona fide Joe's—the one from which all others have sprung."[43] Driving through the Bay Area, it's clear that there are a lot of imitators.

Through the course of my conversation with Marie, I met Nicky—who's been with Original Joe's for forty years and has pictures on the long photo wall documenting the entire history of the family restaurant—and many other longtime employees who have grown up with the place. Pointing to photos of former employees, either long retired or deceased, Marie proudly talked about how so many of them started "from nothing" (like her father) and started at Joe's. "It was an opportunity for so many."

"My father didn't have a vision," Marie said of his initial foray into the restaurant business. "His vision was to not starve." Like many hardworking immigrants to the country, he was simply trying to make a way for himself and eventually his family—and ended up living the American dream.

"It feels gratifying, humbling, happy, joyous," she said when I asked, as she took in all the black-and-white photos on the wall, how it felt to be part of such a long-lasting legacy. "We're going to celebrate our eightieth

DESSERTS

Zabaione (for 1) 60c;		Swiss Cheese	.35
2 or more (each)	.50	Monterey	.35
Fried Cream	.60	Gorgonzola	.35
Ice Cream	.25	Camembert	.35
Pie 20c; a la Mode	.40	Roquefort	.35

Have you tried our world-famous JOE'S SPECIAL $1.35

COCKTAIL SUGGESTIONS

Manhattan	.50	Alexander	.60	Bacardi	.60	Daiquiri	.60
Martini	.50	Domestic Picon	.50	Champagne		Stinger	.60
Old Fashioned	.50	Imported Picon	.75	Cocktail	1.00	Pink Lady	.60
Side Car	.60	Gibson	.50	Dubonnet	.50	Campari Cocktail	.50

WINES (per glass)

Sherry	.25	Angelica	.25	Sauterne	.20
Port	.25	Burgundy	.20	Dry Sack Sherry	.50
		Dubonnet	.50		

BEVERAGES

Tea	.15	Milk	.15	Eastern Beers	.40
Coffee	.10	Local Beer	.25	Splits (Eastern)	.25

Right interior of vintage menu from New Joe's, a now defunct popular Italian restaurant that figures prominently in the "Joe's Special" mythology. *Author's collection.*

birthday this year." It's remarkable to think that a restaurant that opened in the 1930s—persisting through the war years of the '40s, the postwar boom of the '50s and dramatic changes to the neighborhood from the '60s through the '80s and '90s, ultimately experiencing a devastating fire in the early 2000s—is about to mark eighty years young.

San Francisco Chronicle food writer Kim Severson called the restaurant an "improbable survivor" in her wonderful 2003 article about the place and its staying power:

> *Step past two guys sharing a crack pipe on the corner of Taylor and Turk, push open the doors to Original Joe's and take a seat at the long counter.*
>
> *Here, where a mist of grease from frying calamari hangs in the air and massive hamburgers broil over mesquite charcoal, it becomes clear that everything you think you know about San Francisco–style dining is wrong.*
>
> *Forget artisan cheese and baby greens and Dungeness crab, and the lovely cafés in which they are served. This counter is the city's culinary ground zero, baby—a place where cooks slam halibut into blackened sauté pans and tuxedoed waiters whip up zabaglione with cheap Chablis. It's the original Original Joe's, the grandpappy of Northern California's style of eating.*[44]

Severson nails the Joe's legacy and trendsetting achievements in the piece: from the open kitchen (a necessity in the tiny original restaurant) to the mesquite charcoal used in the grill (more affordable in those days) and the locally sourced products; bread from a North Beach bakery, locally caught sole and applewood-smoked bacon all featured prominently in the Joe's experience. Severson says even late-night dining was a thing at Joe's before it was popularized at other later city hotspots.

The counter Severson mentions was the heart of Joe's back in its Tenderloin days, welcoming to all and a place where all members of the San Francisco community—from society types to blue-collar workers—felt at home. Marie was so inspired by the counter culture at her family's restaurant that she wrote a poem about it in 1989, now framed and proudly displayed on the photo wall:

> *There's a counter in the city*
> *In a dicey part of town*
> *It's had clients through the decades*
> *Who've come from all around*

There are judges, cops, and gamblers.
Cabbies, priests, and lawyers too
They all meet at the counter
Over pot roast or beef stew.

It's like the United Nations
In a great reception hall
The counter knows no color,
It respects the green of all.

For a brief time at the lunch hour
Society's pecking order fades
White collars blend with blue ones
As brief alliances are made

It's certainly not the country club
Where impropriety makes them frown
It's just the counter where humanity meets
In a dicey part of town.

I grew up with both New Joe's and Original Joe's, acquainted by my family visits to the city, usually to see a musical or go Christmas shopping in Union Square. I recall the tight squeeze of my hand as my parents gripped it, leading my sister and me through the rough Tenderloin neighborhood of the 1980s to get to the restaurants. But I couldn't wait to get inside: the deep red leather booths, the smell of pasta sauce and the sight of professional, tuxedoed waiters was a treat every time. And the Joe's Special felt like an omelet with the eggs minimized, making it more of a pile of hamburger flecked with green that I was allowed to eat for dinner. Such joy!

My most exhilarating moment of this book was when Marie Duggan ushered me trustingly and assuredly into the restaurant kitchen. "Come on, come right in. It's OK," she assured me, as I dodged swiftly moving back-of-the-house folks prepping lunch entrées and soups, delightful smells all around. "I'm gonna have them make you a Joe's Special. *Celito? Can you make her a Joe's Special, please?* He's made thousands of them. And he makes it best," she said.

Cecelio "Celito" Garcia then smiled from behind a wide prep station, cutting board placed neatly before him, nodded and moved deftly to the right, quickly collecting the ingredients he's come to know over decades of preparing this famous, simple dish. Apparently, the pan at "the old place" (the original location that burned down) was a secret ingredient they can no longer obtain; Marie described it as a "thin black old-fashioned pan—I think it's called a French frying pan," that was not cast iron and not aluminum but a special alloy that was the perfect base for making the Joe's Special. Also, it was never washed—"just scraped clean"—so decades of seasoning had built up to provide a hidden but phenomenal base of flavor to each dish prepared in it. I pinched myself as I watched the dish come together before my eyes, a memory scroll of Joe's Specials eaten throughout my own childhood while tucked into the sumptuous red-leather booths, feeling a part of a fortunate San Francisco club that got to eat a pile of perfectly seasoned and dressed ground beef for dinner. And I can attest, even without the special pan, Celito's Joe's Special was out-of-this-world delicious.

Recipe for a Joe's Special (as I watched it)

Generous knob of butter
¼ cup chopped yellow onion
1 cup (½ pound) ground beef
½ cup cooked spinach (looked to be cooked with a little garlic)
2 eggs
Salt and pepper to taste

Add butter to a hot sauté pan over medium-high heat. Let it begin to melt. Toss chopped onion into the pan; walk away confidently. Return 30 seconds or so later, toss the pan gently to move around the onion. (You may use a wooden spoon or silicon spatula for this as well.) Once the onion has become a bit translucent and golden, add the ground beef. Toss around again to distribute and cook evenly. Cook until the pink meat goes mostly brown; add spinach and toss into the beef mixture. Crack eggs onto the top of the beef mixture individually. Walk away again, confidently, briefly. Give the eggs time to make friends with the beef, but don't let them fry. Return to the pan and work the eggs into the mixture using a wooden spoon until the eggs become like a gentle binder for the whole mess. Season with salt and pepper to taste.

Optional, but a must in my book: Serve topped with sautéed mushrooms (that have been sautéed in butter, garlic and a touch of wine). Serve with either a glass of delicious red wine or a very cold martini—gin, always gin. Please.

North Beach at night (Columbus Café, Pete's signs), 2017. *Author photograph.*

"The Joe's Special is so simple, you could make it," Marie told me confidently when I asked what she loved most about the famous dish. Thank you, Marie; I think I will. And as I do, I will think of the three generations of Rodins (now Duggans) who have kept the Joe's dream alive (Marie's kids John and Elena operate it today). Now the institution sits in the same building where the family patriarch, original owner Tony Rodin, once lived, overlooking Washington Square Park and the North Beach neighborhood that has fostered the burgeoning dreams and endeavors to just make it of so many immigrant groups over the decades.

Chapter 15

AN INSTANT HIT: GREEN GODDESS DRESSING AND THE PALACE HOTEL

(1923)

The green goddess salad is surprisingly not named for its color, though it is a pale green. Invented by a hotel chef for a fancy party honoring an actor in 1923, the dressing—which is what the name refers to, not the composition of the salad it's used on—has persisted in popularity, with peaks and valleys, over nearly a century. Said chef in the origin story was the one presiding over the still-magnificent Palace Hotel kitchen in the early twentieth century, executive chef Phillip Roemer. The occasion was a celebrity gala for actor George Arliss, star of the hit play by William Archer *The Green Goddess*. In the early twenty-first century, the addictive concoction seemed to be enjoying a resurgence in allegiance, popping up on restaurant menus throughout the city and making appearances on special occasions (like my own 2010 wedding). Panera Bread cafés even feature a Green Goddess Cobb Salad (With Chicken) on their menu in 2017. And it is worth the hype.

A perfect foil to crisp greens like romaine or sturdy ones such as kale, green goddess dressing is also delightful with shrimp served in lettuce cups, as they were at my wedding. It's a wonderful accompaniment to roast chicken as a sauce or even as a dip for crudité. It's hard to imagine what it's not good with (frankly, I could even see it with a rich, beefy steak, the perfect counterpoint to all that marbling). There's something irresistible and midcentury about the tang combined with intense creaminess, brightened with densely incorporated herbs. When I eat something with the stuff, I want more and more.

Palace Hotel green goddess salad, original preparation, early twentieth century. *Palace Hotel.*

Recipes vary, but all have herbs and a creamy white ingredient in common (typically, sour cream and mayonnaise). Half of the duo who has created a fervor for classically made yeast-leavened bread in the city, Liz Prueitt, wife to baker Chad Robertson, co-founders and owners of the growing Tartine empire, contributed a recipe for her version of the tangy dressing to online cooking blog Food 52.[45] She incorporates avocado, anchovies and chopped carrot tops, along with classic ingredients such as sour cream, mayonnaise and a whole host of herbs (heavy on the tarragon, which she describes as a "woefully underused herb").

Celebrity chef Tyler Florence's Wayfare Tavern on the edge of the Financial District in the city has, since its opening, paid tribute to classic San Francisco dishes. In 2010, *San Francisco Chronicle* restaurant critic Michael Bauer covered the revival of the original green goddess dressing in a salad at Wayfare,[46] noting that it was based on the recipe provided by Julie Murray, granddaughter of Roemer. Though Roemer died in 1936, his family reportedly maintained his recipe collection, composed of dishes he made at the Palace and presumably instructed in the cooking classes he taught. Bauer reports that he was also a contributor at the late *San Francisco Call* newspaper.

My favorite versions of the salad and its famous dressing vary with the day of the week and the occasion. I adored the preparation at my wedding by phenomenal Oakland restaurant Pizzaiolo, in the dense, vibrant, restaurant-and-small-business-loving Temescal neighborhood in the north part of the city. Wayfare's reverence to the classic is delightful, though subtle, but ideal seated at the chef's counter, watching the open kitchen, classic cocktail in hand. For a majestic experience at the place where it all began, you can't beat brunch in the Garden Court at the Palace Hotel, amid opulent chandeliers, soaring ceilings and well-dressed hotel patrons sipping champagne and clinking china. Renee Roberts, who has been with the hotel for two decades doing public relations and more, says that when the dish was first introduced, long before her time, of course, it was "an instant hit."

"We believe it's because of its bright, herbaceous flavor that complements vegetables, seafood and poultry beautifully," she says. "The vibrant color from the fresh herbs is also very appealing. When it was first created, that was unusual for salad dressing. Even today, you don't see many dressings that are vivid green."

Agreeing that the dressing has become a favorite of "celebrity chefs and trendy restaurants," Roberts sums up its popularity: "Green goddess has a creative origin, has been a steady favorite for decades and is simply delicious with a variety of foods."

Courtesy of the Palace Hotel, two recipes follow. Note that the modern version drops the sour cream and prepared mayo but involves a homemade prep for the latter and diversifies the herbs. Murray's recipe, as printed with permission in the 2010 *Chronicle* article, looks more like a blend of these two versions from the hotel. It's hard to say which is more accurate—the Palace files or the granddaughter's family archives—but for the purposes of preparing and enjoying the delightful dressing, it makes no matter.

Palace Hotel Original Green Goddess Dressing (1923)

1 cup mayonnaise
½ cup sour cream
¼ cup snipped fresh chives or minced scallions
¼ cup minced fresh parsley

1 tablespoon fresh lemon juice
1 tablespoon white wine vinegar
3 anchovy fillets, rinsed, patted dry and minced
Salt and freshly ground black pepper to taste

Stir all the ingredients together in a small bowl until well blended. Taste and adjust the seasonings. Use immediately or cover and refrigerate.

Palace Hotel Green Goddess Today

1 tablespoon fresh minced tarragon
1 tablespoon chopped chives
½ cup fresh minced parsley
2 finely minced green onions
3 cloves minced garlic
2 tablespoons chopped white onion
2 minced anchovy filets
2 egg yolks
3 tablespoons tarragon vinegar
1 ½ teaspoons lemon juice
2¾ cups olive oil
Salt and pepper to taste

Combine all ingredients except olive oil, salt and pepper. Using a traditional or immersion blender, blend until smooth. While blending, slowly add olive oil in a steady stream until dressing begins to thicken. Add salt and pepper to taste. Makes 3 to 4 cups.

According to the Palace, a version of the green goddess salad has been on the menu since the dressing was created in the early twenties, though the original salad was a product of limited access to fresh ingredients, so the dressing was served with shredded iceberg lettuce, canned vegetables and a choice of chicken, shrimp or crab. In 2017, it's the Garden Court Signature Crab Salad that bears the green goddess dressing and features farm-fresh baby greens, locally grown vegetables and "a generous portion of Dungeness crab meat." With Dungeness season right around the corner as I write this (early winter), my mouth is positively watering.

Chapter 16

CULT OF COOKIES AND CREAM: IT'S IT

(1928)

When a 1920s-era amusement park–born ice cream treat suddenly comes in a green tea flavor, it's pretty clear the product has kept pace with the times. Such is the case with the It's It, the beloved ice cream sandwich featuring oatmeal cookies and a cloak of rich dark chocolate, a legendary treat born at Playland-at-the-Beach, a ten-acre amusement park adjacent to San Francisco's Ocean Beach that eventually closed in the early '70s, to the dismay of kids across the city. The treat, however, remains manufactured locally to the pride and delight of generations of Bay Area residents. Vanilla was its original flavor, and over the years, it was joined by a modest group of others, including chocolate, mint (the best), cappuccino (second, sometimes first, best), strawberry, pumpkin and the newest, green tea.

The iconic ice cream sandwich was invented in 1928 by George Whitney, owner of Playland and the Cliff House, with his brother Leo. Legend has it that he was working to develop the perfect ice cream treat for patrons of the park, to be sold at his ice cream and sandwich shop, when he finally pressed two oatmeal cookies around a scoop of vanilla ice cream, dipped the whole thing in chocolate and proclaimed, "That's it!" The Playland stand dedicated to selling the new treat was marked with a "This is IT" sign and sold hamburgers and milkshakes along with the treat that outlasted even the park itself.

Still family-owned, but by a different family—the Shamiehs—since the 1970s, It's It is now headquartered just south of the city in Burlingame. The addictive treats are both made and sold right on the premises, the

Ocean Beach and the Great Highway, 1917, *Album of San Francisco*, A3, vol. 1, p. 325. *California History Room, California State Library, Sacramento, California.*

Playland owner George Whitney took over the nearby Sutro Baths in 1952, managing the famous swimming pools and amusement area until 1966. *San Francisco History Room, San Francisco Public Library.*

sales operation courtesy of a fairly new addition to the site: the company's "Factory Shop." Mostly locals frequent the store that feels like a typical ice cream scoop shop, only instead of frozen containers of ice cream beneath the glass case, there are large, cold bins full of individually wrapped ice cream sandwiches. The benefit of visiting lies in the dependability of the full assortment of flavors—except on rare occasions when they've run out of something, like, on my visit, chocolate—because a new batch is always scheduled for production the next day. Visiting the headquarters location also means there are special offerings not typically available at your corner liquor store or supermarket (where It's It is strategically sold in the area). Exclusive products include the It's It Sundae, which looks like a frozen banana but is simply, straightforwardly, vanilla ice cream wrapped in dark chocolate and rolled in chopped peanuts. "It's plain but my absolute favorite," the shop girl told me when I inquired about it. The Big Daddy was another surprise: a square of vanilla ice cream sandwiched between two thin chocolate wafers, rather than oatmeal cookies, and minus the cloak of chocolate.

"Kids like it a lot," Lana Shamieh explained. Daughter of one of the handful of owners—all in the family—and a company employee herself of five years, Lana said she enjoys working for the family business. Because of my project, she deftly packaged up an entire case of It's Its for me—that's twenty-four ice cream sandwiches—along with adorable T-shirts for my kids. They will wear them with pride—allowing me to pass along my own childhood addictions to the next generation.

Lana's uncle and current It's It company president Charles "Charlie" Shamieh is one of a handful of family owners who bought the company in the early 1970s after the city tore down Playland and the ice cream company went up for sale. At the time, the Shamieh family owned and ran a pizza and ice cream shop themselves, along with a liquor store, on Castro Street. And they made their own family version of the It's It using Mother's brand oatmeal cookies and good local ice cream. They called it Jamal's Old-Fashioned Ice Cream Sandwich after one of their kids—but patrons would always come in and ask for an It's It, Shamieh recounts. When the Shamiehs heard the original was up for sale, they knew they had to buy it.

Eventually moving from a 1,500-square-foot production facility on Eleventh Street in San Francisco to a now 17,000-square-foot facility south of the city, the Shamiehs have shepherded the iconic treat through the decades, preserving the purity and everything-from-scratch qualities that have made it so great—and doing practically no advertising.

"It's all word of mouth, really," Charlie Shamieh explained, as did his nephew Paul, attorney by education and marketing guru, part of the younger generation who operates the company today. That generation, though, is doing a superb job harnessing fans' passion for the product on social media, creating hashtags for the few new product launches they've done in recent years and encouraging people who visit the factory shop—or social channels—to share their love of It's It online. They also purposely

Eva Whitney, mother of George Whitney, and kids on a roller coaster at Playland at the Beach, San Francisco. *San Francisco History Center, San Francisco Public Library.*

follow a somewhat counterintuitive business model: they don't want their product everywhere. Paul admits that something that makes It's It special is that you can't find it everywhere, so when it pops up at your corner market, it's exciting.

Importantly, the Shamiehs still make everything in house today. They buy milk and cream from a local co-op (with products solely from Northern California) and process the dairy themselves. They conduct their own heat pasteurization very slowly, taking the milk from 39 degrees Fahrenheit to 165 degrees Fahrenheit over several hours for what they claim is the best-tasting product. After that, they homogenize it, also in house, heating under pressure to make the texture "really smooth and creamy," and then place it in a cooling tank to bring it back down to around 40 degrees. At this point, they add the flavors—for instance, adding cocoa for the chocolate or coffee granules for the delectable cappuccino flavor—mixing them for a full twenty-four hours before cookies are added like bookends and the creation

Postcard of Ocean Beach showing the Joy Zone at Playland on the left, looking down on the Great Highway from Sutro Heights. *California History Room, California State Library, Sacramento, California.*

passes through a series of other machinery: a spiral tunnel, an enrober (for the chocolate) and a cooling tunnel.

The quality of the ice cream depends on how much air you put into it, Charlie Shamieh explained to me. "A lot of air makes for a lower-quality product, while less air makes for a creamier, more dense ice cream."

Why is It's It still a hit in 2017, I asked Charlie. Three reasons, he said: great quality; a catchy, fun name; and its long-standing place as a San Francisco tradition since 1928. His pride in being a part of the legacy is clear. "Honestly, besides having a company and making a good living out of it, growing year after year…it's really an honor to keep that tradition. Because if we hadn't taken it over, it would have died."

Locals' devotion to It's It manifests in myriad ways, ranging from expected and countless personal anecdotes of generations of fans and when they had their first It's It—how their grandfather or great-grandfather introduced them—to an entire wedding cake made of It's Its.

Charlie Shamieh enthused, "Some people say, 'Rice-A-Roni isn't the San Francisco treat, it's It's It!' We agree!"

As I pondered the concept of a family of Palestinian immigrants saving from loss and keeping alive a beloved ice cream sandwich at an amusement park, such a quintessential American treat, I realized something. It was the Shamieh It's It I'd grown up with. The It's It of my own childhood was theirs—the only It's It I've ever known. I suddenly felt grateful, acknowledging that this man I was interviewing had given me a part of my own childhood. Charlie was just in his mid-twenties when he bought the company with his brothers, a young man with a degree in electronics but not a lot of opportunity to put that to use. "There were a lot of engineers at the time flipping hamburgers," he says. He took up a couple of small businesses, and then opportunity knocked. He made a decision that has not only led to a prosperous business life but also to a legacy notch in his belt—how he helped save a piece of San Francisco history for future generations. He and his relatives made it possible for modern pastry chefs like Emily Luchetti to have an iconic summertime treat to riff on in their own kitchens.

Luchetti's success spans books, television and a slew of popular local restaurants that expertly capture the sensation of being both glamorously electric and comfortable at once, including Marlowe, Petit Marlowe, Park Tavern and Leo's Oyster House. She developed her own beautiful take on the It's It a few years ago for a feature in the *San Francisco Chronicle* and agreed to share it here.

It's It, collection of flavors. *Brandon Borrman.*

"It's unique, as it combines three of our favorite desserts into one: oatmeal cookies, ice cream and chocolate," Luchetti says. "The fact that it was created in 1928 and still popular in its original version in 2017—eighty-five years later—is a testament to its deliciousness. When I made my version, I wanted to acknowledge and pay tribute to the original but also show people how to make a homemade one."

Luchetti's path to pastry began after college, when she started cooking to pay the bills and fell in love with the industry. She made the switch from savory to sweet after working the line for seven years. "I couldn't peel onions without crying A LOT. It's a little hard to gain respect as a chef if you're bawling your eyes out. I switched to the sweet side and never looked back."

After thirty years in the San Francisco culinary world, she's excited to see it still evolving. "Today, more than ever, there is a wide range of types of cuisines, styles of dining and interesting chefs and restaurateurs, all adding to the richness of the city's cuisine. What is wonderful, too, is how tight and familiar the food community is. We all want to be the best but want our colleagues to be too."

Her sunny picture of the food industry in a fast-paced, ever-changing, tech-dominated metropolis surprises me a bit but is lovely and inspiring. I like to think it's because she works in impossibly cheery mediums like ice cream, cookies and chocolate.

It's-It Revisited, courtesy of Emily Luchetti
Makes 5 ice cream sandwiches

Ginger ice cream
1 cup heavy cream
¾ cup milk
⅓ cup sugar
1 2-inch piece gingerroot, halved
1 2-inch piece of vanilla bean, split
4 large egg yolks
Large pinch salt

Oatmeal cookies
6 tablespoons butter, at room temperature
½ cup firmly packed brown sugar
2 tablespoons granulated sugar

1 large egg
½ teaspoon vanilla extract
½ cup all-purpose flour
¾ teaspoon cinnamon
Scant ½ teaspoon baking soda
⅛ teaspoon kosher salt
1 cup old-fashioned oats

To assemble
6½ ounces bittersweet chocolate

For the ice cream: In a heavy-bottomed pot over medium heat, heat the cream, milk and half the sugar with the gingerroot and vanilla bean until scalded—hot but not boiling; set aside. In a medium-size bowl, whisk together the yolks, salt and remaining sugar. Slowly whisk the hot liquid into the eggs a little at a time, stirring as you pour. Return the mixture to the pot and cook over medium-low heat, stirring constantly with a wooden spoon or heat-resistant rubber spatula, until the mixture reaches 175 degrees or coats the back of the spoon. Strain into a bowl and cool over an ice bath to at least room temperature. Refrigerate at least 4 hours or overnight. Churn in an ice cream machine according to manufacturer's instructions.

For the cookies: Preheat oven to 350 degrees. Beat butter and sugars until smooth and creamy. Add the egg and vanilla extract. Stir in the rest of the dry ingredients and oats and mix just until combined. Using 2 measuring tablespoons for each cookie, roll batter into balls and place several inches apart on parchment-lined baking sheets (they'll spread significantly, so you'll need two sheets). There should be 10 cookies. Bake until brown, 10–12 minutes. Cool to room temperature.

To assemble: Make 5 ice cream sandwiches using a scoop of ice cream and two cookies. Place back in the freezer while you melt the chocolate.

To finish: Melt chocolate over a double boiler. Cool slightly; you do not want it to be hot, but it should still be loose. Transfer the chocolate to a small bowl wide enough to fit the ice cream sandwich. One at a time, dip into the chocolate, coating half the sandwich. Place on parchment-lined baking sheets and freeze until the chocolate hardens.

Chapter 17

NEIGHBORLY CONTRIBUTION FROM ACROSS THE BAY: THE MAI TAI

(1944)

You have to drive along a narrow strip of road that juts out into the San Francisco Bay to reach the home of the original mai tai. Excuse me, the Original Mai Tai®. Choppy brown water slaps against itself on your left, with a weird, massive, 1960s apartment complex called the Watergate on your right. A small driveway opens up just past the apartments, leading to the old-school palace of tiki in the Bay: Trader Vic's.

Supportive, affectedly loud and affectionate millennials surrounded me on my latest visit, "Awwwwooooooh, this is so cute!" "OOH! Punch bowls! Those are like fish bowls!" And, "I just want like a smoothie that has rum in it."

This window into the world of tiki after-effect—or tiki for the masses or the devolution of the mai tai, as Smuggler's Cove founder and tiki subject matter expert Martin Cate might call it (more on that later)—is fascinating. And actually, it's well connected to the origins of the drink that spawned it all—exotic, lovable, sour and sweet, frivolous, making someone say silly things.

"Oh, I love tart. Like, tart things. You know?" one of the millennials—I realized half of a set of twins—enthused.

So, the drink: the 1944 Mai Tai is marketed as the Original one (even trademarked that way), served with crushed ice, a healthy wedge of squeezed lime pushed ever so slightly into the drink and a hearty sprig of mint standing proudly atop the glass's edge. The taste of orgeat, a French almondy gum syrup, is what hits your tongue first, quickly followed by the rums—more than one, I think, but the recipe is a protected secret—orange liqueur (curacao or Cointreau) and lime. It's a lovely combination, one that understandably has spawned many variations over the years.

"The beauty of the mai tai is that it's very simple—and that's where the genius lies in the drink." Though I'd enjoyed a good mai tai on probably dozens of occasions before working on this book, Cate gave me the first clinical download on the cocktail.

"The key wizardry to this drink is that it's unabashedly a wonderful rum cocktail," Cate explained. "It's basically a showpiece for really outstanding rum, and everything dances around it. You've got rum, lime and sugar. The holy trinity. Rum and rum's two best friends."

It's the foundation for a daiquiri or planter's punch, Cate espoused, and given Victor "Trader Vic" Bergeron's French roots and his parents' ownership of a French grocery store, his awareness of orgeat—what Cate describes as Vic's "killer ingredient"—made for a game-changing concoction.

The legendary origin story goes that the mai tai was invented by Bergeron, a San Francisco restaurateur, at the service bar in the Felix Hotel. His socialite

Trader Vic's mai tai in 2017. *Author photograph.*

friends Carrie and Easton "Ham" Guild, who also had a home in Tahiti, came in and asked for something special. Bergeron pulled down a bottle of Wray & Nephew seventeen-year-old rum, 100 percent Jamaican pot still rum, "elegant, oaky, full bodied," says Cate. Bergeron gave the cocktail to Carrie, who then exclaimed, "*Maita'i roa ae!*" which means in Tahitian "Out of this world!"

And it is.

Naturally, though, no super-famous drink worth its notoriety has a clean origin story; this one is disputed. Don the Beachcomber—former restaurateur and barman in Los Angeles, and widely considered to be the godfather of the tiki bar (even Bergeron described him as an inspiration)—claimed to have invented the drink eleven years earlier, in 1933. But there is no evidence that supports that claim—no evidence of the drink on a menu before 1944, that is. And in a lawsuit between Don the Beachcomber's syrup-making operation and Bergeron over the mai tai name, the latter prevailed, supported by Carrie Guild's testimony to her role in the origin story.

Whatever the truth, the cocktail is stupendous. My favorite version is my husband's: heavy on the orgeat and lime, served in an elegant lowball glass with heft. But the Trader Vic's original is pretty great, too.

The lightness in treatment of the place is perfectly tiki, perfectly mai tai.

"Yeah, fun! Funfunfun! Ooooh!" the young friends in Emeryville in 2017 say. "I might just have to do low key, 'cuz I have to do stuff all day with my mom. Then we might do bars, like marina bars and stuff."

"This place is soo cute. I. Obsess. I really think. It's. Adorable."

Dying to know what they'll order.

"I want deep-fried pickles. MMMMMMM. Yummy. You know pickle juice is good for your muscles? When they're crampy? Yeah."

The original Trader Vic's moved in 1971 from Oakland to its present home in Emeryville, which I call "the shopping town" because besides Pixar's headquarters and some interesting converted lofts, it's mostly stores: big box, smaller chains, stadium movie theater and everything in between. But the mai tai is still going strong here. Across that choppy water in the city, the modern mai tai is celebrated, honored and riffed on at Smuggler's Cove, founded in 2009 and already recipient of the James Beard Award, named on countless national and international "best bars" lists and one of the only bars I know of that names its staff members—the owners, all the bartenders and barbacks, administrative support and even the security guard—on its website. Founder and tiki guru Martin Cate described to me his first attraction to the world of tiki, by way of a Trader Vic's in Washington, D.C.

"It's one of those things where it just had a special resonance in a way that a lot of other restaurants or experiences didn't have for me," he reminisced. "It was this discovery of what felt like an alien world, this sort of lost kingdom that used to dot the American landscape in the midcentury. It's a really fascinating thing that gives you a sense of freedom, of escape, but also of shelter and coziness and all the things that come with a great tiki bar that make you feel far more relaxed and at ease than most places."

After first visiting Trader Vic's, Cate built a home tiki bar, eventually hosting parties, coordinating a "tiki weekend" in San Francisco and later becoming a bartender at the San Francisco outpost of Trader Vic's in 2004, the same year it reopened after a ten-year hiatus from the scene. Cate describes the relaunch of what was once a glorious, see-and-be-seen location that had hosted in 1981 Queen Elizabeth, Prince Philip and Ronald and Nancy Reagan for the queen's first meal not prepared by a palace chef as a "big mistake," full of "hubris."

"They just couldn't put the genie back in the bottle. They thought, 'All of our old regulars will be back, and they'll be all excited to taste the classics again.' Unfortunately, the average age of a Trader Vic's regular was dead."

Cate opened Smuggler's Cove in 2006. And he lives the commitment, serving like a walking, talking history book to the life and times of tiki drinks and classic cocktailing the world over. (Though you may find him sipping a beer in his downtime rather than a navy grog or a zombie.) His poetic description of what the initial tiki bar experience offered is transportive:

These places offered an escape in the 1950s from the kind of relentless go-go American progress that was pushing forward through the space age and midcentury boom time of postwar economic success in America. They offered a real contrast to this sleek chrome, to the futuristic, to the sense of constant forward motion. To go somewhere that was made of natural materials and woven burlap thatch and palm cane. That you could escape both the pressures of your job, of society, of the sort of fear of nuclear apocalypse during the Cold War, all the things that you were looking to hide from.

They offered a sense of shelter without having to travel very far. It was the place where you could loosen the tie and take the hat off, and sip deeply of a wonderful beverage, and listen to some soft, trickling water and some gentle music playing in the background. You really had something.

Cate's recounting of the early days of the tiki craze is positively enchanting. It resonates with modern American pressures and the forces pushing citizens toward an escape hatch, making me wonder why there isn't a tiki bar on every corner in 2018.

For his contribution to the pantheon of sheltering bars, Cate chose a nautical theme, focusing the bar's decor on "ephemera of South Seas commerce, shipping crates, barrels, fishnets and floats," in honor of both San Francisco's maritime heritage and "the maritime traditions of rum."

The Tonga Room at the Fairmont Hotel, of course, cannot go without mention as an example of both a historic and modern spot to enjoy a mai tai in the city of San Francisco. Replete with a band on a floating stage, oftentimes conga lines and an insta-party atmosphere, the Tonga Room is keepin' it real in the tiki category after nearly three-quarters of a century. It feels both current and vintage at once and is an irresistible place to try an original mai tai in the style of Vic Bergeron; the bar even describes it on its menu as "an East Bay classic."

Some tiki bars, however, offer more than one kind of mai tai: Trader Vic's style and a Hawaiian version, the latter believed by some to be a bastardization of the pure original, taking on pineapple juice and a float of rum, at a minimum—additional tropical juices and amaretto in a blend that strays far from the original, straightforward conceit of the drink. The Hawaiian take hails from Matson steamship history; there used to be a cruise line that ran between San Francisco and Oahu, Cate explained to me. Important to note: Trader Vic himself was hired as a menu consultant on the route. Naturally, he made sure to export his mai tai, which eventually took on Hawaiian flavors of its own.

And on the east side of the bay, Forbidden Island in Alameda (also an island) and the Kona Club in Oakland offer respectable, delightful versions. Both establishments offer both the original and Hawaiian-style mai tais, the latter with the addition of pineapple juice and a dark rum float; Forbidden Island describes its Island Mai Tai as like "a *Brady Bunch* tropical vacation in a glass!" These cocktails, however, tend to take a backseat in focus to all the grogs and punches offered at Forbidden Island and to the Kona house special, the Macadamia Nut Chi Chi (essentially a boozy, nutty milkshake that knocks the socks off unsuspecting guests). Both bars are lovely little neighborhood joints, private, not showy, with dullish exteriors that mask the secret getaway sensation held within. Just like good tiki bars should. Highly recommended.

Before we conclude our Polynesian journey around Bay Area bars—the mai tai trail, if you will—we shall go back to where it all begin, both the chapter and the mai tai itself: Trader Vic's. Returning to our millennial friends in Emeryville, the drink's history seems not even a blip on their collective consciousness. But they are having a great time. When the one male member of the party received his drink, after an upswell of oohs and aahs about how pretty it was—a dusty rose color in an oversized coupe, adorned with a fresh white flower—the three girls stopped talking, whipped out their cameras and tried to get the perfect picture. This continued for several minutes, each member of the party competing to get the better shot.

Festive, enthusiastic, appreciative of the beauty and artistry and whimsy of this sort of cocktail and the light, vacation-like vibe the moment evoked, it was perfectly tiki. And like any good exotic cocktail, I'm certain the moment was more complicated than it seemed. Importantly: It. Was. Adorable.

Smuggler's Cove Mai Tai

Cate's recipe, featured at his wonderful bar, is adapted from the Trader Vic's original and included in his book Smuggler's Cove: Exotic Cocktails, Rum and the Cult of Tiki (by Martin Cate and Rebecca Cate, Ten Speed Press, 2016). Editor's note: While Cate goes to the trouble of making his own orgeat, Berkeley-based Small Hands Foods, a Bay Area local just a few miles from where the mai tai was born, makes a fantastic, fantastically purchasable version. (We have a bottle in our home fridge at all times.)

"Within the pantheon of exotic cocktails, one stands above the rest as the most iconic of the era. An elegant and simple concoction, really just a nutty rum margarita, it eschews the conventional structure established by Don [the Beachcomber] in favor of a more nuanced approach."—Martin Cate

Glassware: Double old-fashioned glass

¾ ounce fresh lime juice
¼ ounce SC Mai Tai Rich Simple Syrup*
¼ ounce orgeat (see editor's note)

½ ounce Pierre Ferrand dry curacao
2 ounces blended aged rum
Garnish: Spent lime shell and mint sprig

Combine all ingredients with 12 ounces of crushed ice and a few cubes in a cocktail shaker. Shake until a frost forms on the shaker and pour the entire contents into a double old-fashioned glass. Garnish with a spent lime shell and mint sprig.

*SC Mai Tai Rich Simple Syrup (makes 4 cups)

2 cups water
4 cups demerara sugar
½ teaspoon vanilla extract
¼ teaspoon salt

Bring the water to a boil in a saucepan over high heat. Add the demerara sugar and stir vigorously with a whisk (or use an immersion blender) until the sugar is dissolved, about 1 minute (the water should become clear such that you can see the bottom of the pot). Immediately remove from heat and let cool. Add the vanilla extract and salt and stir to combine. Pour into a lidded bottle or other sealable container and store in the refrigerator. The syrup will keep, refrigerated, for several weeks.

Chapter 18

BREAKFAST OF CHAMPIONS: IRISH COFFEE

(1950s)

A note on the images in this chapter: Something is so striking about the historic versus the modern: the modern-day versions all seem like near-exact replicas of the circa 1950s originals! This shows how true to its original concept and ambiance the BVC has remained...and how those Irish coffees are the gift that keeps on giving when it comes to a high-octane pick-me-up.

You must cross the cable car tracks to step into the Buena Vista Café, situated at the corner of Hyde and Beach Streets, on the edge of the city, between Fisherman's Wharf and the expanse of Fort Mason, with the bay stretching out before you and the Golden Gate Bridge in your sights. The scent of chocolate sometimes permeates the air, emanating from adjacent Ghirardelli Square with its famed chocolate company (and a slew of other food businesses and retail shops) and glowing sign dominating the waterfront. The sound of seagulls and rumble of the cable cars reaching their terminus provide a constant soundtrack. And there are throngs of tourists everywhere you look. I mention all this to say: there's a lot going on right outside the café, but once you step inside the humming joint, with a glass of Irish coffee sitting on the bar before you, warming your bones, alleviating your worries and soothing your soul, you'll want to stay forever.

"Ah, this is how every parent should start off in the morning," my husband said on our last visit. Our kids full of wiggles, anxiously awaiting breakfast and overall on the verge, parental stress suddenly dissipated, covered by the

Cover of vintage Buena Vista Café menu. *Author's collection.*

boisterous activity and spirit of camaraderie fostered by communal tables and, well, the fact that everyone is drinking a blend of coffee and booze at all hours of the day.

The house elixir is both a pick-me-up and calm-me-down, apropos for any occasion, with any drinking companion, at any time, deep and sharp and creamy and easy all at once. A blend of only coffee, Irish whiskey, cream and a touch of sugar, it's hard to believe that there's even a recipe for the drink—or that there was any trouble in settling on a combination and technique that worked for its preparation.

But legend has it that there was.

First, though, we should pay respect to what came before the legendary drink. The Irish coffee wasn't the first boozy caffeine drink popular in San Francisco. Clarence Edwords includes in his *Bohemian San Francisco* (1914) a recipe for "Coffee Royal" amid "A Few Rare Recipes," which the author describes as such: "In our travels through Bohemia it has been our good fortune to gather hundreds of recipes of new, strange and rare dishes, prepared by those who look farther than the stoking of the physical system in the preparation of foods….From our store we have selected the following as being well worth trying."

His surprisingly complex description of a Coffee Royal goes:

Take of the best Mocha coffee one part, of the best Java coffee two parts. Put six tablespoonfuls of the mixture into a bowl and add an egg, well beaten. Stir the mixture five minutes. Add half a cup of cold water, cover tightly and let stand several hours. Put into a coffeepot the coffee mixture and add four large cups of boiling water, stirring constantly. Let it boil briskly for five minutes only then set on the back of the stove five minutes. Before serving add a small tablespoonful of pure French brandy to each cup. Sweeten to taste.

From this eggy, liquor-tinged coffee drink evolved the Irish coffee, though the latter was not expressly a variation on the former. Rather, it came nearly forty years later from Ireland by way of a *San Francisco Chronicle* travel writer, Stanton Delaplane, who allegedly liked the whiskey coffee drink he had in the Shannon Airport so much he wanted to bring it to his home city. Legend goes that Buena Vista Café owner Jack Koeppler and Delaplane worked through the night of November 10, 1952, mixing and tasting and adjusting and retasting, struggling with the flavor and a cream that would sink to the bottom of the glass each time. It was only through a trip back

Buena Vista Café, circa 1950s. *California Historical Society, Buena Vista Cafe records, 1932–1984, MS 4132.*

to Ireland (by Koeppler) and intervention by the then mayor of the city, George Christopher, who also owned a dairy, that they found success.

"It was discovered that when the cream was aged for 48 hours and frothed to a precise consistency, it would float as delicately as a swan on the surface of Jack's and Stan's special nectar," states the café's history.

I know what you're thinking. Aged cream? But it doesn't mean soured, just not direct from the cow to the cocktail glass. And the drink is a perfect creation. To watch the longtime bartenders at the Buena Vista make a dozen at a time, lined up down the bar like little soldiers, is a zenlike spectator's sport. They work rapidly and calmly and I'm sure could do it in their sleep, given the couple thousand Irish coffees they make daily. Testament to the popularity of the drink and professionalism of its makers, the Buena Vista Café even holds the Guinness World Record for making the largest Irish coffee ever concocted: in 2008, the record-setting drink contained ten liters of whiskey, four pounds of sugar, ten gallons of local Peerless coffee and two gallons of lightly whipped cream. They even tapped the glass so all the spectators could taste victory.

Bars across the city list Irish coffee on their menus, but the best place to get it is at the source. International devotees and local regulars pour in daily to the 1916 saloon—with noticeable boosts on the weekends—and customers are single, couples, families, young, old and some even just begun (newborns in strollers or carriers are not rare sights here). The communal tables impart an immediate sense of friendship and same side–ness that sometimes feels so lacking in America today. Go for the coffee cocktail but get food too; the Dungeness crab omelet in season, with Swiss, heirloom tomatoes and a side of perfectly spiced house potatoes and two huge hunks of grilled sourdough toast, is a positive delight.

And of that cocktail. Pictures, though plentiful and drool worthy, just don't do it justice. In person, the cream floating on top is a stark white and looks impossibly light, like a fluffy cloud awaiting an angel's rest. The ratio of coffee to sugar to booze feels scientific; any more or less of any one ingredient and it wouldn't be a San Francisco Irish coffee. And its warmth is a powerful draw. There's something about hot drinks that feels simultaneously illicit and completely appropriate, like a fifth food group that only comes into play at cold-weather holidays. My favorites are the ones with dairy: hot buttered rum and the drink of the moment, the Irish coffee. My husband and I were reminded so much of our love for the drink on our last visit to the Buena Vista that we've decided to serve it on Christmas morning to our guests. If there's a better way to bring local cheer, honor our history and soften the edges of life's at-times sharp responsibilities, I can't imagine it. Like our own grownup Christmas miracle.

Buena Vista Café's Famous Irish Coffee

Fill an Irish coffee glass with very hot water to preheat, then empty it. Pour hot coffee into hot glass until it is about three-quarters full. Drop in 2 cocktail sugar cubes. Stir until the sugar is thoroughly dissolved. Add a jiggerful of Irish whiskey (be sure it's Tullamore Dew) for proper taste and body. Top with a collar of lightly whipped cream by pouring it gently over a spoon. Enjoy it while piping hot.

Chapter 19

MISSION BURRITO:
OF THE NEIGHBORHOOD, TO THE WORLD

(1960s)

I've never known a world without burritos. As a child growing up in Northern California and then a college student exploring life on her own in the southern part of the state, burritos were ever present, ever delicious and ever diverse. My mom made smallish (compared to Mission burrito standards) home-cook ones with ground beef, shredded cheddar or Monterey jack cheese and refried pinto beans from a can. Sometimes there were olives or sour cream, and oftentimes, Mom's—and friends' moms'— burritos came in the form of an enchilada-style casserole dish, covered in red sauce and more cheese and likely baked at 350 for thirty-five minutes. And other exhilarating times, Mom—and then my sister and I in her footsteps— made a lunchtime burrito, featuring only a hot dog and cheese wrapped in flour tortilla and microwaved for twenty seconds on high. I am not ashamed. But the tradition does reveal something important in how we defined a burrito: it contained meat and cheese, at a minimum, wrapped in a flour tortilla—always flour.

The smothered burrito is something I got to know in college from Alberto's, a popular burrito stand in Santa Ana that has since proliferated into restaurants across the region. Basically, it was a Mission-style burrito— which means an overstuffed, gigantic flour tortilla, featuring meat, beans, cheese, rice and salsa; but more on that later—covered in ranchera sauce and termed "wet." Not possible to eat with one's hands, the wet burrito dictated a knife and fork treatment. Alberto's also claims to be the originator of the California burrito, which features avocado and French fries in place of rice.[47] (I have so loved this variation intermittently over the last twenty-plus years and, most recently, subsisted on a version of it from a local food truck in the Bay Area through two pregnancies.)

So we know this much: burritos are widely believed to be delicious. Burritos are mostly handheld—with some exceptions. Burritos have both Mexican and American roots, and their variations are seemingly endless in this century. But who claims them? And what is this "Mission" version associated uniquely with San Francisco?

In his 2012 *Saveur* article[48] "Burritos Unwrapped: The Curious Evolution of a Borderland Classic," Gustavo Arellano traces the path of the burrito from Mexico to the United States. In the piece, he documents the signature family road trip for him and his parents, through the "borderland" area of northern Mexico on a route along Highway 45—in modern years plagued by drug wars—documenting the food's murky history. In the town of Ahumada, he sets the scene:

> *Here, roadside stalls, sit-down restaurants, and street vendors sell burritos of every stripe—vegetarian (*rajas con queso, *chiles with cheese); spiced ground beef called* picadillo; *even hot dogs stewed with salsa, hilariously known as* burritos de weenie—*all rolled into a flour wrapper folded in such a way so that the ends are not tucked in, better to portion out the bites with filling and those of pure tortilla.*

His parents, he shares, made distinctions between these and the American versions of the food:

> *The burrito to them was as alien as a Korean taco; being from Zacatecas, where corn tortillas are the norm, they hadn't even tasted the flour variety until migrating to California in the 1960s. The American obsession with the food bewildered them—the ones we ate in the States were as Mexican as Doritos. But in Villa Ahumada, my parents were happy to feed on burritos because, well, that's what everybody ate. To them, Ahumada was the place where America became Mexico, and Mexico became America; the burrito was the food that embodied that in-between place.*

Arellano talks about how the burrito originated in Mexico—in its purest form—and how it has become so Americanized that "all sorts of gastronomic sins get committed in its name." He also clearly outlines the distinction between the American and Mexican versions of the food:

But in the borderlands of Mexico, the burrito has reigned for nearly a century as a simple, austere beauty reflective of its sparse environment. It's here that the meal reaches its apotheosis, not as a tortilla wrapped around an avalanche of mush, but as a dish in which each part complements the others: an expertly toasted flour tortilla, with just enough filling so that it can be tightly wrapped to the girth of a child's wrist. The ideal iteration is more graceful than gargantuan.

More gargantuan than graceful, the Mission burrito is claimed by several local taquerias to be their baby. Culinary historian Erica Peters traced its origins in the specific way of a true academic, giving credence and credit to different outlets for their contributions. Here's what Peters outlined about her assessment of the origin story:

1949: Al Williams' Papagayo Room served a normal-sized burrito
1961: El Faro sold extra-large burritos
1969: La Cumbre sold extra-large burritos, made via assembly line
1973: La Taqueria (at 2889 Mission) opened
1979: Patricia Unterman explains the dish to Chronicle *readers*

Unpacking that, Peters first points to a 1949 advertisement in the *San Francisco Chronicle* for the Papagayo Room at the Fairmont Hotel, with the following menu item: "Burritos: rolled tortillas with shredded beef, served with sour cream ($1.35)."

Thirty years later, legendary food writer Patricia Unterman defined the dish in a 1979 *San Francisco Chronicle* article called "El Burrito—The All-American Food Item from Mexico."[49] Her straightforward, exceedingly simple, explanatory writing is a reminder of the value of a good description. It sounds like she's writing about something that's not offered on every corner—and in 1979, it wasn't, at least not in the way it is nearly forty years later. Brevity and plainness are a beauty here:

A burrito, for those of you who aren't sure, is a Mexican meal wrapped up in a flour tortilla and tinfoil. It costs anywhere from $1.20 to $1.80, here in San Francisco, and consists of Mexican red beans, rice, cooked meat of some sort, salsa which is a relish that may contain onions, tomato and coriander, and something very hot. A typical burrito is shaped like a fat sausage, weighs anywhere from a third to three quarters of a pound and feels warm in your hand.

Unterman goes on to discuss both La Taqueria (at 2889 Mission) and La Cumbre (at 515 Valencia) but doesn't address the question of origins, as Peters pointed out to me.

John Roemer's "Cylindrical God" article in *SF Weekly* on May 5, 1993, involves original research, including an interview with Charlene Aguilar, at the time assistant director of the Center for Chicano Research at Stanford University, and, in turn, her interview with her own grandfather, Antonio Aguilar, and subsequently various market and deli owners in the Mission dating back to the 1960s. Roemer talks about how El Faro is the place widely believed to have served the first "Mission" burrito—named for the Mission district, the neighborhood in which it all happened—in 1961. Febronio Ontiveros was the owner, and as Roemer says, the story goes like this:

> *The first retail burrito in San Francisco, it can be stated with some confidence, was made and sold on September 26, 1961, exactly one day after Ontiveros and his wife opened a corner grocery store at 2399 Folsom Street.…Ontiveros said that on the first day he was open, a group of firemen from a station down the street came in wanting sandwiches. He didn't have any, but the industrious businessman wouldn't disappoint them twice. The next day he was ready with burritos. Soon he made them a staple of the store's growing takeout trade. There were no big tortillas commercially available in those days, so to make the super burrito he overlapped three six-inchers and charged a dollar.*

But if you visit the Mission or read anything about the origins of its famous burrito today, another name frequently pops up: Taqueria La Cumbre on Valencia Street. Roemer addresses this locale, too, describing the city's purported "oldest taqueria" and its "spicy but simple burritos." Peters says that La Cumbre, opened in 1969, is known for inventing the assembly-line approach to preparing the fat burritos, though there doesn't seem to be a definitive written source to prove it (other than the bright red "Birthplace of the Mission-Style Burrito" banner out front). This "Mission Local" article from 2017 describes the opening of La Cumbre:

> *La Cumbre's story began in 1967, when Mexican immigrants Raul and Michaela Duran opened a meat market at 515 Valencia Street, the site of a former vaudeville theater built in 1908. Seeing that blue-collar workers needed a substantial yet portable meal, the Durans created what*

Taqueria La Cumbre, claimant to being the birthplace of the Mission burrito, Mission District, San Francisco, 2017. *Brandon Borrman.*

is now known as the Mission burrito—served assembly-line style with rice, beans, meat, cheese, and vegetables, and wrapped in an oversized tortilla.[50]

Roemer quotes owner Raul Duran in his *SF Weekly* article, describing him as "a confirmed traditionalist," meaning that things at La Cumbre are pretty much the way they were fifty years ago: a smattering of simple tables, a blend of traditional Mexican artwork and instruments and San Francisco tchotchkes on the walls and straightforward burrito ingredients.

My favorite parts of La Cumbre—other than the fact that almost no one working there speaks English—are the obvious pride taken in product and the salsas. Not unlike modern taquerias, there's a self-serve salsa bar off the main counter. Go cautiously if spice concerns you, and ask for advice from those in the know. I did and fell hard for the two green salsas with my deluxe chicken burrito (carnitas is the more traditional, fatty beaut, but I was feeling poultry that day). Both tomatillo salsas, one is cooked, featuring roasted tomatillos, and the other is served raw, blended with avocado— best portioned generously, bite by bite, for maximum flavor throughout the experience.

John Birdsall's brilliant 2016 piece in *Bon Appétit* magazine documents both the alleged origins and modern fervor around the Mission burrito, explaining how the birth of a chain restaurant dedicated to the dish has changed our perceptions about its perennialness. Before Chipotle, Birdsall points out, there wasn't a fat, overstuffed burrito known nationwide. Importantly, Birdsall shares a detail I hadn't known before: the founder of Chipotle, Steve Ellis, lived in San Francisco and worked at Stars, Jeremiah Tower's European-style see-and-be-seen city hotspot in the 1980s. In 1993, Ellis took the beloved signature San Francisco neighborhood burrito from the City by the Bay to the world with his first Chipotle outlet in Denver. "Within a month that shop was selling more than a thousand Mission-style burritos a day."[51]

San Francisco Chronicle food writer Jonathan Kauffman has covered certain otherwise uncovered culinary subjects prolifically—case in point, his *Hippie Food: How Back-to-the-Landers, Longhairs, and Revolutionaries Changed the Way We Eat* (William Morrow, 2018). I love what he says about the Mission burrito and am inclined to print word-for-word our exchange on the subject, but one must be selective. He was definitive about his favorite burrito:

> *Considering that La Altena (spit-cooked al pastor) burned down two years ago, I have two favorites, both involving carnitas, which is the only and perfect burrito filling. Neither of them is a hidden discovery: La Taqueria, though it's almost heretical in eschewing rice, and El Castillito on Mission and Seventeenth. Runner-up: Taqueria San Francisco on Twenty-Fourth Street.*

And what makes a Mission burrito? "To my mind, it's girth and rice," Kauffman says. And on this point, we agree: "The presence of lettuce immediately disqualifies a Mission burrito from being a Mission burrito."

There's only one burrito I can recall not liking in my entire life, which is saying something about my openness to, and patience with, variations of the food. It was recently, at a fancy grocery store fresh-food counter. It should have been great but was the opposite: flavorless, bland and not worth the calories. But it was just that one. Kauffman, however, says he's eaten so many burritos in his life that he's developed "an intolerance" for bad ones. "Salsa that's all onion and no flavor, charred meat, lettuce [see above]. The central flaw of a mediocre-to-bad burrito is bad rice; a lot of cheap taquerias add it for filler, but it has to be strongly seasoned so it doesn't suck up all the flavor of the meat and leave you bored after three bites."

Strongly seasoned, belly filling, soul satisfying and diverse, the Mission burrito is a real expression of its birth neighborhood. Born in a time of free love and antiwar and vibrant artistic expression—the murals of the neighborhood are brilliant, signature features—the Mission burrito speaks both to its heritage and the modern circumstance of the neighborhood. There is an actual mission in the area, Mission Dolores, originally Mission San Francisco de Asis, founded by Catholic priests in the late 1700s and now purportedly the oldest structure in San Francisco itself, while the neighborhood is experiencing a new demographic change, growing less Latino and more hipster. But all the while, the burrito persists there, taking new forms, the classics fighting for their place in modern popularity and history. I will let Jonathan Kauffman eloquently close out this thought on why the Mission burrito is a legacy food of the City by the Bay:

> *It expresses a historic era in the formation of San Francisco—specifically, the transformation of the Mission into a Mexican and then Latino neighborhood in the 1950s to 1980s—and then the way that the Mission became an essential part of the city's own self-perception. The fact that the burrito isn't true to anything you'd eat in Mexico and doesn't really resemble burritos in Los Angeles, San Diego or Texas is what makes it so distinctively an expression of here.*
>
> *The fact that San Franciscans get smug and combative about their burritos warms my heart.* [So true. And the people getting combative are from all walks of life: young, old, rich, poor, Mexican, Caucasian, you name it.]
>
> *At the same time, to me the burrito also tastes of a time that is almost lost, as the Mission's Latino population shrinks and the Mission has become something other than what it was.*

And on the evolution of this famous food? "I love that the burrito has become a canvas for tons of other San Francisco cooks to paint on with Filipino, Jamaican and Indian flavors. I just can't get with the sushirrito, however. That thing is gross."

Chapter 20

THE PERFECT CLOSE TO A NIGHT—OR A BOOK: TOSCA'S HOUSE CAPPUCCINO

(1919)

The only cappuccino I know that has not a drop of caffeine, Tosca Café's infamous house cappuccino has been warming the chests and souls of San Franciscans since 1919. The concoction with a kick is pretty unique—and uniquely San Francisco—and provides the perfect way to wind down after a long day of work (or long night of partying) in a style that feels like a warm hug.

"It's my favorite thing to drink in the city," my friend Cori Tahara says of the cocktail. After an impressive tenure working with some of the most acclaimed chefs and food industry folks in California, she should know what's worth sipping.

As one white-jacketed bartender told us on a recent visit, "There's no caffeine whatsoever. It's just like a boozy hot chocolate."

Here's how the conversation between Cori, my husband and me went after our first sip on said visit:

Cori: Oh, I love that drink so hard.
Me: That *is* boozy.
Brandon: Not bad…

The drink is so delicious, the only challenge is to stick with just one. As with the notorious Chinese mai tai of the Li Po Lounge, a few blocks over from Tosca, more than that could hurt.

Bar at Tosca Café, 2017. *Brandon Borrman.*

Longtime North Beach bar Tosca Café became famous for its many famous patrons through the Beat era and into the 1980s and '90s, from filmmakers and rock stars to poets, politicians and movie stars. Customer Sean Penn purportedly helped save it from permanent closure in 2012 when a back-rent issue threatened its existence altogether. Penn contacted restaurateurs Ken Friedman and April Bloomfield back in New York (best known for their wonderful gastropubs the Spotted Pig and the Breslin, the latter being the site of one Thanksgiving meal for my own family). Within months, they took it over.[52]

The bar is now a full-blown restaurant as well, serving up addictive and expertly prepared Italian food by now Bloomfield and her team alone (Friedman exited after much-publicized sexual harassment allegations against him in 2018), in a space that feels both new and nicely worn-in. The bar itself feels comfortable, lived in, loud but simultaneously private. There's a depth to sitting there, taking in the flurry around you and pondering all the night owls who did the same thing over the century before you. It's easy to understand the appeal.

I asked the Tosca team about the history of the special drink made famous there. They took me back to Prohibition-era San Francisco. Here's how head bartender Eric Stashak described it:

Tosca closed down momentarily when Prohibition hit San Francisco and reopened as Tosca Café to keep up appearances. Around this time, they began serving their "house cappuccino," which provided a way for patrons to subtly get their alcohol fix, as the drink was essentially a spiked hot chocolate. It allowed Tosca to continue on as a neighborhood hang, with the added allure of one of the (not so few) places in town where one could still get a drink.

Fascinatingly, the elixir hit the city about thirty years before Irish coffee but is significantly less well known.

As the team noted, "It continues to baffle people today by being caffeine free.…Today, we have a good mix of people ordering it for nostalgia's sake, as well as by newcomers that are drawn to its exceptional taste and a younger crowd that orders it simply because of its popularity and legend."

The drink itself is the stuff of legend and has changed over the years just a bit. Historically, hyper-local Ghirardelli chocolate was used in the recipe, but as San Francisco chocolate companies have proliferated over the years, the current Tosca team features a different, still local, modern product. Today's version also diversifies the booze, with both bourbon and Armagnac, a personal favorite. And over the years, it has spread beyond Tosca's walls—evidenced by its feature with seeming monastic roots on the spine of a midcentury menu for New Joe's restaurant, the famed Italian joint that is part of the Joe's lore (see chapter fourteen on Joe's Special).

A wonderful 2013 article by Mickey Rapkin in *Bon Appétit* magazine documents Tosca's phoenix-like rise from the near ashes and asked some of its famous patrons about the cocktail. "The House Cappuccino was the thing to order," said actor Dennis Quaid. And industry peer Laurence Fishburne responded, "Those coffee drinks? Insane, man! The best." Former legendary owner Jeanette Etheredge described the drink as "Ghirardelli chocolate and milk, steamed in the machine, with the addition of a shot of brandy." When asked how many are sold each night, she said, "I have no idea. They're lined up on the bar."

Tosca's Famous House "Cappuccino"

4 ounces whole milk
2 ounces chocolate ganache*
½ ounce Wild Turkey 101 Bourbon
½ ounce Chateau Lebaud Armagnac

Luscious "house cappuccino" at Tosca Café, 2017. *Brandon Borrman.*

Steam milk. Create as much foam as possible and set the foam aside.

Heat the chocolate ganache until it is at a temperature that is too hot to touch. (This can be done in a microwave gingerly, at a medium power, or gently on the stove using a double boiler.)

Mix the bourbon and armagnac with the hot chocolate ganache. Combine the steamed milk and chocolate-booze together; stir until incorporated.

Top with a dollop of the milk foam and serve.

*Chocolate ganache is easy to prepare at home—and an easy way to impress your guests with your culinary fanciness. Prepare chocolate ganache by pouring very warm heavy cream over chopped bittersweet chocolate in a one-to-one ratio for a thick but still spreadable consistency. Add a pinch of salt. Once chocolate has begun to melt under the warm cream, whisk the cream into the chocolate so the two become one. Unless using immediately, keep refrigerated (ganache should last about a week).

NOTES

Introduction

1. Coloma, "California Gold Discovery," www.coloma.com/california-gold-discovery.
2. History, "The Gold Rush of 1849," www.history.com/topics/gold-rush-of-1849.
3. Ibid.
4. Tracing the Truth, "Before the P.P.I.E.: The Mechanics' Institute and the Development of San Francisco's Fair Culture (1857–1899)," tarynedwards.com/2016/02/19/before-the-p-p-i-e-the-mechanics-institute-and-the-development-of-san-franciscos-fair-culture-1857-1899.
5. Tracing the Truth, "Healthful Fermented Liquids at the Mechanics' Institute's Industrial Exposition, Part I," tarynedwards.com/2014/08/19/healthful-fermented-liquors-at-the-mechanics-institutes-industrial-expositions.

Chapter 1

6. Erica J. Peters, *San Francisco: A Food Biography* (Lanham, MD: Rowman and Littlefield, 2013), 189. Citing Walter Colton, *The Land of Gold or: Three Years in California [1846–1849]* (New York: D.W. Evans, 1860), 298.
7. Ibid., 189.

8. YouTube, "SF Sourdough Episode 3, Steven Sullivan, Founder of Acme Bread," www.youtube.com/watch?v=Pg6wr9KTtNU.

9. Christine Muhlke, "America's Most Influential Bakery Is Only Getting More Influential," *Bon Appétit*, April 6, 2017, www.bonappetit.com/story/tartine-americas-most-influential-bakery.

10. Susan Reid, "Josey Baker and the Mill: Fresher Than Ever," King Arthur Flour, January 25, 2016, blog.kingarthurflour.com/2016/01/25/josey-baker-mill.

Chapter 2

11. Barbara Maranzani, "8 Things You May Not Know about the California Gold Rush," History Stories, January 24, 2013, www.history.com/news/8-things-you-may-not-know-about-the-california-gold-rush.

12. "Kräusening" is the process of adding a proportion of active wort to cellar tanks containing fully fermented beer. The term "kräusen" refers to wort when it is at its most active state of fermentation.

Chapter 4

13. Leah Bhabha, "The History of the Martini," Food52, May 16, 2014, food52.com/blog/10396-the-history-of-the-martini.

14. Emma Janzen, "The Martinez Gets Its Groove Back," *Imbibe*, September 12, 2016, imbibemagazine.com/martinez-cocktail-comeback.

15. Bull Valley Roadhouse, www.bullvalleyroadhouse.com/menu-test.

Chapter 5

16. Bill Addison, "Mister Jiu's Is a Love Letter to America's Oldest Chinatown," Eater, May 12, 2017, www.eater.com/2017/5/12/15627340/mister-jius-review-san-francisco-brandon-jew.

17. Peter Smith, "Was Chop Suey the Greatest Culinary Joke Ever Played?" Smithsonian, March 12, 2012, www.smithsonianmag.com/arts-culture/was-chop-suey-the-greatest-culinary-joke-ever-played-122173708.

18. L.L. McLaren, *Pan-Pacific Cook Book: Savory Bits from the World's Fare* (San Francisco: Blair-Murdock Co., 1915).

19. Sam Wo, "Our Family Story," www.samworestaurant.com/our-family-story.

Chapter 6

20. McLaren, *Pan-Pacific Cook Book*, 21.
21. Tablehopper, "Fishermen's Grotto No. 9 on the Wharf Has Reopened with a Fresh Look and Update," www.tablehopper.com/chatterbox/fishermens-grotto-no-9-on-the-wharf-has-reopened-with-a-fresh-look-and-update.
22. Food & Wine, "Judith's Dungeness Crab Cioppino," www.foodandwine.com/recipes/judiths-dungeness-crab-cioppino.

Chapter 7

23. Gary Kamiya, "Forbidden City Ushered in Golden Age of Chinatown Nightclubs," *SFGate*, January 9, 2015, www.sfgate.com/bayarea/article/Forbidden-City-ushered-in-golden-age-of-Chinatown-6005033.php.

Chapter 8

24. Carol Jensen, *Byron Hot Springs* (Charleston, SC: Arcadia Publishing, 2007).
25. David Wondrich, "Masters of Mixology: 'Cocktail' Bill Boothby," Liquor.com, July 22, 2013, www.liquor.com/articles/masters-of-mixology-cocktail-bill-boothby.

Chapter 9

26. Nicole Martinelli, "High Spirits," The Bold Italic, thebolditalic.com/high-spirits-the-bold-italic-san-francisco-3c3715ccdaa3.
27. "The Montgomery Block, a warren of studios, galleries, courtyards, and saloons at Washington and Montgomery—the so-called Monkey Block—once favored by artists, writers, and bohemians." Matthew Stafford, "Pisco Punch, a Butt-Kicking Sip of S.F. History," *SF Weekly*, October 8, 2009. archives.sfweekly.com/foodie/2009/10/08/pisco-punch-a-butt-kicking-sip-of-sf-history.

Chapter 10

28. Veronica Meewes, "Reinventing the French Cure-All: DIY Amer Picon," PUNCH, March 25, 2015, punchdrink.com/articles/reinventing-the-french-cure-all-diy-amer-picon.

29. Trader Vic, *Bartender's Guide* (Garden City, NY: Doubleday and Company Inc., 1947), 352.

30. Stephen Schwartz, "Basque Traditions Are Fading Away in S.F./North Beach Eatery Is Latest Casualty," *SFGate*, December 27, 1996, www.sfgate.com/news/article/Basque-Traditions-Are-Fading-Away-in-S-F-North-2954630.php.

31. Andrew Meltzer, "Picon Punch," PUNCH, punchdrink.com/recipes/picon-punch.

Chapter 11

32. Food52, "Old School Chicken Tetrazzini," December 29, 2013, food52.com/recipes/25565-old-school-chicken-tetrazzini.

33. Genius Kitchen, "Creamy Turkey Tetrazzzini," www.geniuskitchen.com/amp/recipe/creamy-turkey-tetrazzini-57505.

Chapter 12

34. Barbara Hansen, "Paying Homage to a Legendary Chef of the Past: Victor Hirtzler of Hotel St. Francis Established San Francisco's Dining Style," *Los Angeles Times*, August 25, 1988, articles.latimes.com/1988-08-25/food/fo-1005_1_san-francisco.

35. Peters, *San Francisco: A Food Biography*, 176.

36. Victor Hirtzler, *The Hotel St. Francis Cook Book* (Chicago: Hotel Monthly Press, 1919), 330.

37. McLaren, *Pan-Pacific Cook Book*, 111.

38. Clarence Edwords, Bohemian *San Francisco: Its Restaurants and Their Most Famous Recipes; the Elegant Art of Dining* (San Francisco: Paul Elder & Company, 1914), 63.

Chapter 13

39. Peters, *San Francisco: A Food Biography*, 182–83.
40. Tamar Adler, "Return of the Sun King," *New York Times Magazine*, June 30, 2016, www.nytimes.com/2016/07/03/magazine/return-of-crab-louis.html.
41. Omar Mamoon, "Secret Recipe: Swan Oyster Depot's Classic Combination Salad," 7x7, October 16, 2015, www.7x7.com/secret-recipe-swan-oyster-depots-classic-combination-salad-1787236215.html.
42. Andrew Knowlton and Julia Kramer, "America's Best New Restaurants 2016," *Bon Appétit*, August 9, 2016, www.bonappetit.com/story/best-designed-restaurants-2016.

Chapter 14

43. Kim Severson, "Eat at Joe's/In San Francisco, All Roads Lead to This Tenderloin Original," *SFGate*, August 13, 2003, www.sfgate.com/recipes/article/Eat-at-Joe-s-In-San-Francisco-all-roads-lead-2301478.php.
44. Ibid.

Chapter 15

45. Liz Prueitt, "Greenest Goddess Dressing and Dip," Food52, May 5, 2017, food52.com/recipes/70642-greenest-goddess-dressing-and-dip.
46. Michael Bauer, "Wayfare Tavern Revives the Original Green Goddess," *SFGate*, November 14, 2010, www.sfgate.com/food/chefssecrets/article/Wayfare-Tavern-revives-the-original-green-goddess-3246160.php.

Chapter 19

47. Alberto's Mexican Food, www.albertosmexfood.com.
48. Gustavo Arellano, "Burritos Unwrapped," *Saveur*, August 10, 2012, www.saveur.com/article/Travels/Mexico-American-Burritos.
49. Patricia Unterman, *SF Chronicle*, December 23, 1979.

50. V. Alexandra de F. Szoenyi, "Taqueria La Cumbre Celebrates 50 Years in the Mission," Mission Local, May 3, 2017, missionlocal.org/2017/05/taqueria-la-cumbre-celebrates-50-years-in-the-mission.
51. John Birdsall, "The Story of the Mission Burrito, Piled High and Pulled Tight," *Bon Appétit*, October 11, 2016, www.bonappetit.com/restaurants-travel/article/burrito-october-feature.

Chapter 20

52. Mickey Rapkin, "Tosca Café: The World's Best Last Dive Bar," *Bon Appétit*, May 14, 2013, www.bonappetit.com/restaurants-travel/article/best-last-dive-bar-in-world.

INDEX

ABOUT THE AUTHOR

California native Laura Smith Borrman is a writer, editor, story gatherer, lover of food and drink and author of two previous books about the culture and culinary landscape of the Bay Area. She has worked in many industries, spanning pastry kitchens, culinary travel, public radio, research and the corporate world, and loves sharing people's stories. She's also a mother of two and lives with her husband and children in Oakland. She writes about the city's classic business landscape and the people who have shaped it at discoveringvintagesanfrancisco.com and about food memories, recipes and motherhood at cravingsofhome.com.

Visit us at
www.historypress.com

CPSIA information can be obtained
at www.ICGtesting.com
Printed in the USA
LVHW080400210219
608282LV00002B/8/P